BRIDLEWAYS

of Britain

Wiltshire riding country above the Wylye valley.

BRIDLEWAYS

of Britain

Long distance routes for
weekend and holiday rides

Introduced by

Elwyn Hartley Edwards

WARD LOCK

First published in 1991 by Ward Lock
Villiers House, 41–47 Strand, London WC2N 5JE, England
125 East 23rd Street, Suite 300, New York 10010, USA
A Cassell imprint

British Library Cataloguing in Publication Data
Bridleways of Britain
    1. Great Britain. Bridleways. Description &
    travel
    I. Hartley Edwards, Elwyn, 1927–
914.1′04858

    ISBN 0–7063–6786–3

Produced by Antler Books Ltd.
Reference section and maps by Charles Jacoby.
Typeset by Footnote Graphics, Warminster, England.
Jacket origination by J Film Process Ltd.
Printed and bound in Singapore.

Riding is a potentially hazardous pastime. The
information in this book is intended to provide a
general, but not specific, guide to some of the areas of
Britain where Bridleway Riding may be enjoyed. The
authors and publishers have undertaken diligent
research, but they cannot accept responsibility for
information which may be incorrect. They strongly
advise those intending to ride the routes described to
seek further information; and they suggest that
anybody who writes to any of the addresses given in
the book should enclose a stamped addressed envelope
for a reply. Furthermore they accept no liability for
any accident or damage caused by or to those who
ride the bridleways described.

Contents

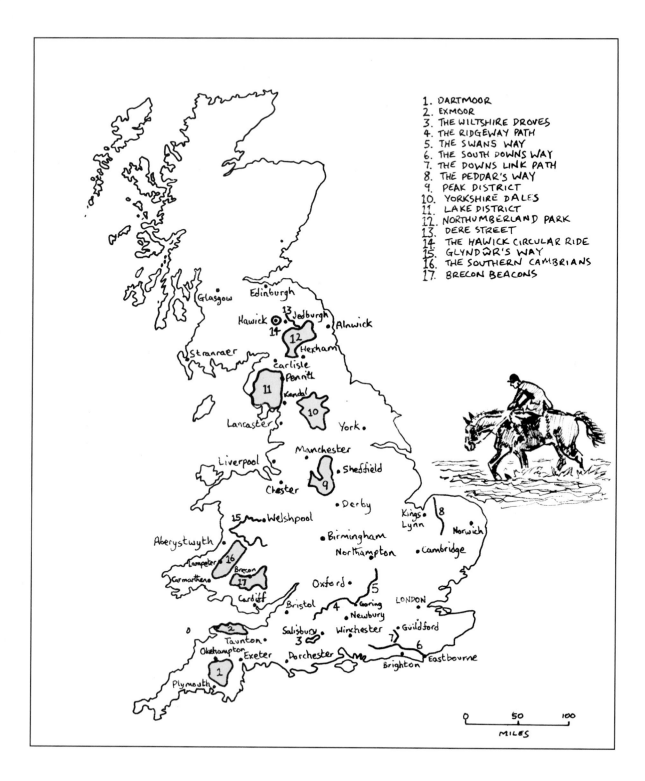

1. DARTMOOR
2. EXMOOR
3. THE WILTSHIRE DROVES
4. THE RIDGEWAY PATH
5. THE SWANS WAY
6. THE SOUTH DOWNS WAY
7. THE DOWNS LINK PATH
8. THE PEDDAR'S WAY
9. PEAK DISTRICT
10. YORKSHIRE DALES
11. LAKE DISTRICT
12. NORTHUMBERLAND PARK
13. DERE STREET
14. THE HAWICK CIRCULAR RIDE
15. GLYNDŴR'S WAY
16. THE SOUTHERN CAMBRIANS
17. BRECON BEACONS

Preamble

The tradition of long-distance riding is as old as the association of Man and Horse. It began as a matter of necessity and continued as such certainly right up to the turn of the century, whilst in some parts of Europe horses remained integral to the economy well into the period between the two World Wars, providing the principal source of mobility.

Today's horsemen and women, despite their ability to travel half-way across the world in less than 24 hours, continue the tradition of distance riding. If they do not exactly follow the dictum of King Alfred, who when he was not burning cakes exhorted his contemporaries to 'ride forth singing', they take to the horse for the pleasure to be found in sharing a journey through the countryside in company with the animal being which, arguably, made the greatest contribution to the human condition. Others, motivated by the spur of competition, pit themselves and their horses against time and terrain in rides demanding inexorably of the qualities of stamina, endurance, speed, courage and most importantly, of horsemastership.

Without doubt, modern competitive rides are comprehensive tests in all these respects. Whether they can be compared with the performances of the past, many of which in the context of their time would have been regarded as no more than commonplace, is a matter more open to argument.

Riding up to the Long Mynd near the proposed Shropshire Horse Way. (Picture courtesy of Tom Linfoot)

There is little or no record of the feats performed by the world's first horse peoples of the Asian steppes, but much more is known of the Mongol hordes of Genghis Khan who in blood and pillage carved an Empire from the backs of their tough and enduring steppe ponies and created that 'Pax Mongolica' which was to provide a base for later and more culturally active societies. Napoleon made a serious study of the Mongol tactics and over 130 years later generals of World War II, notably Rommel and Montgomery, were still practising the classic Mongol *tulaghma*, the 'standard sweep' that turns an enemy's flank so as to take him in the rear.

Modern riders could, indeed, learn from the management techniques imposed on 'the hordes' (under penalty of death) by Genghis Khan, whose numerous titles include that of 'the Perfect Warrior', which in respect of his capabilities as a commander of cavalry was not too far from the truth. They might, however, draw the line at the nomad custom of carrying their meat ration under the saddle or even in the seat of their breeches. Samuel Butler (1612–1680), author of *Hudibras*, had a neat little verse to describe the practice:

> . . . his countrymen the Huns
> Did stew their meat between their bums
> And the horses' backs whereon they straddle,
> And every man eats up his saddle!

The Khan maintained a sophisticated system of communications throughout the sprawling Mongol Empire by means of the *Yam* (the prototype of the American Pony Express). Relays of couriers galloped along the caravan tracks carrying the orders of the Khan and his *Orkhons* (the divisional commanders). Each man, changing ponies at the gallop, rode 150 miles (242 km) a day and we have to presume that they thought no more of that than did the Khan's principal commanders, Chepe Noyan and Subutai Bahadur, when they were summoned from the banks of the Volga for consultation with the Khan in the homeland of the Gobi Desert 2,000 miles (3,220 km) away. They completed the journey in a month and then rode back in the same time. Something less than 400 years later Sir Robert Carey rode from Windsor to Edinburgh bearing the news of Queen Elizabeth's death to her successor James Stuart. He completed the 400 miles (650 km) in 66 hours.

America's legendary Pony Express, inaugurated by William H. Russell in 1860 to carry the mails between Missouri and San Francisco, made its own special contribution to endurance riding as well as to the heroic image of the 'frontier spirit'. 400 ponies, ridden as hard as they could lay legs to the ground, completed the 1,966 mile (3,164 km) journey in ten days, less than half the time taken for the epic journey of Messrs. Chepe and Subutai. The fastest run ever was made by 'Pony Bob'

A Peak District bridleway alongside the river Dove.

Haslam who covered the 120 miles (193 km) from Smith's Creek to Fort Churchill in eight hours ten minutes. However, he did have the incentive of being pursued by bands of scalp-hungry Indians.

These rides, though achievements of a formidable stature, were, however, made using relays of horses, as were the very famous rides, often made for wagers, of Count Sandor and the English Squire Osbaldeston. The former once rode the 230 km from Buda to Vienna in nine hours ten minutes at an average speed of 26.5 kph, whilst Osbaldeston rode 200 miles on a circular track in nine hours.

The first organized one-man-one-horse rides, the forerunners of the modern competition rides, were those staged in the 1890s and early 1900s by European cavalry, particularly that of Germany and the Austro-Hungarian Empire. Supposedly, these were military exercises designed as tests for man and horse with the object of improving standards. In the event they were races of inhuman severity with the horses being literally ridden to death. They earned the sport a reputation of cruel exploitation which was to persist into relatively recent times. One of the most infamous was the 1892 Berlin–Vienna ride of 580 km. It was won, at the cost of his

An ancient packhorse bridge over the river Wye in the Peak District.

horse's life, by Count Starhemberg, in 71 hours 27 minutes. Within days some 25 horses had died of their exertions. The Paris–Deauville ride of 1903, organised by the journal, *Armes et Sport*, was possibly the first to impose limited speed restrictions in the interests of the horses' welfare, but it was the American cavalry which introduced the first supervised rides which were to become the blueprint for competitive distance riding.

In 1919 the U.S. Cavalry conducted endurance tests to assess the respective qualities and the suitability of Arabian and Thoroughbred horses as remounts. The horses were required to cover the 300-mile course in five days, travelling 60 miles per day and carrying weights between 200–245 lb. Great emphasis was placed on improving the standards of horsemastership in the field and the rides were carefully overseen with this object in view.

The 1936 Vermont 100-Mile, a three-day ride, one of the first American civilian events, derived directly from the military tests and from that point the sport in America developed rapidly, encouraging the formation of numerous Trail Ride Associations. America now stages upwards of 500 rides each year including the toughest test of all, the famous 100-mile Western States Trail Ride, more popularly known as the Tevis Cup Ride. It began in 1955 when Wendell T. Robie with four companions set out to prove that modern horses were just as enduring as the cow-ponies of the American pioneers which had blazed the Pony Express trail.

The ride is from Tahoe City, Nevada, to Auburn, California and follows the steep, hazardous trail over the Sierra Nevadas. The total aggregate descent faced by the riders is no less than 15,250 ft and there is also the awesome 9,500 ft climb through the snowbound Squaw Pass which leads on to El Dorado Canyon where temperatures can reach over 100 degrees. There are very stringent veterinary checks at intervals over the whole course and the entry is limited by qualifying rides. The distance is most usually covered in times varying between 11–12 hours and all who complete within the limit of 24 hours are awarded the famous silver and gold buckle. An additional award, the Haggin Cup, is awarded to the fittest finishing horse of the fastest ten.

The Australian equivalent, which is almost as demanding in terms of the country to be ridden over, is the Tom Quilty Endurance Ride over the same distance, whilst South Africa stages a three-day ride, the South African National Endurance, over a longer distance of 130 miles. In these rides, as well as in the major events held in Britain and other parts of Europe there have been some remarkable performances, though it is doubtful whether any can approach the feat of the horses which completed the ride from Ashkabad to Moscow in 1935. These were a group of Akhal-Teke and Iomud horses, breeds renowned for their endurance under the harshest climatic conditions, and they covered the 2,580 miles in 84 days. For 600 miles the route crossed desert lands and for much of the journey water was in short supply.

In Britain distance riding was pioneered by the Arab Horse Society, and like nearly all horse sports their early 'endurance races' were run in furtherance of the cavalry horse. The Arab, above all other breeds, is the world's supreme long-distance horse and the big distance events are dominated by Arabs and their close derivatives. The Society first organized endurance races in the 1920s, the declared object being '. . . to demonstrate to the War Office the phenomenal stamina and recuperative powers of the breed, with a view to an infusion of Arab blood into the cavalry horse'. The horses in those rides, none of which would have been over 15 h.h., carried 13 st. and as with the U.S. Cavalry trials were expected to cover 300 miles in five days.

The Arab Horse Society still stages an annual Marathon over the classic distance of 26¼ miles (42 km) and a testing course which, despite a compulsory walk section of just over a mile, is a race, the first past the post being the winner. It is unique in the field of British distance riding and so is the other Arab Horse Society innovation the Ride and Tie which originated in America with the Levi Ride and Tie Race first run in 1971. The race is run with one horse and two riders. One rides a certain distance, dismounts and tethers the horse and then runs on. His colleague runs to where the horse is tied, mounts and rides away. He, in turn, having overtaken his partner, dismounts and ties the horse, going off on foot again and so on.

Competitive long-distance riding in Britain really began with the 100-mile rides organised by *Country Life* and *Riding* magazines in 1937 and 1938. The finish was at Eastbourne, competitors having the option of riding one of the eight routes within a 100-mile radius of the town. The maximum distance covered in a day was 300 miles and there were control and veterinary check points. Medals were awarded to those completing the ride.

After World War II, the *Sunday Telegraph* sponsored Britain's first Golden Horseshoe Ride over Exmoor. That was in 1965; three years later the Ride was run jointly by the Arab Horse Society and the British Horse Society. Since 1975 the BHS Long-Distance Riding Group has been responsible and the Ride has always been held over the beautiful but challenging Exmoor routes.

The Golden Horseshoe is a 100-mile final ride, held over two days, for which horses and riders must have qualified by competing in less severe rides of 40 miles at a speed of 7.5 mph. It is not a race. Gold medals are awarded for those completing the course at not less than 8 mph and who pass the strict veterinary examinations. Silver and bronze are awarded on the basis of speed and veterinary penalty points.

The Long-Distance Riding Group runs a number of other rides, the Cotswold 100 and the Goodwood International 100 being endurance rides which unlike the long-distance rides are to all intents races, although run under strict rules and penalties designed to safeguard the horse's well-being.

The Endurance Horse and Pony Society, formed in 1973, is the other British society. It differs from the LDR by basing its rules on the American system. It runs *Pleasure Rides, Competitive Trail Rides* and *Endurance Rides*. A *Pleasure Ride* acts as an introduction to the sport and is well within the capacity of the average rider who might think of riding parts of any of the long-distance bridleways described in this book. It takes place over distances of 10–25 miles at a minimum speed of 5 mph, which is no faster than a leisurely hacking pace. The LDR Group organises similar rides and, like those of the EHPS, veterinary supervision is not required, although it may sometimes feature in the organization.

Competitive Trail Rides represent the middle level of the sport and their rules are probably the most complicated. Essentially the rides take place over marked routes which in the novice division may be between 20–25 miles, the distance being covered in this instance at between 6–7 mph. Veterinary penalties may be incurred for pulse, respiration rates etc outside the stated parameters. Open trail rides are over longer distances and have to be ridden at higher speeds (25–60 miles at between 7–8 mph) and there are also some faster rides (8–9 mph) over 25–35 miles. The same penalties apply.

Endurance Rides are races over 50–100 miles, the distance to be completed in one

Dartmoor riding country near Hexworthy.

day. The principal EHPS event is the 100–mile Summer Solstice Ride held in the New Forest and designated the British Open Endurance Riding Championship.

European national societies belong to the European Long Distance Rides Conference (ELDRIC), a body which organizes the European Trophy, a competition based on a points system. Intenational events, The European and World Championships, are run under the rules of the Fédération Equestre Internationale (FEI) and there has to be a possibility of the sport being included in the Olympic disciplines within the foreseeable future.

Recreational Riding

Competitive long-distance riding has a large and enthusiastic following but surveys show quite conclusively that the most popular activity is just hacking in the countryside. Increasingly, too, more and more people want to extend their daily or weekly hack into rides over longer routes with the possibility of viewing a different part of the country. This is what the long-distance bridleway provides whilst adding a sense of purpose and achievement to a riding holiday.

Before the advent of the motor-car people used horses and, of course, bridleways, to get about their business. John Wesley, for instance, led the Methodist revival of the 18th century from the back of a horse, travelling an estimated 8,000 miles a year in the saddle. William Cobbett's *Rural Rides* (1830), a picture of the changing world of the early 19th century, was made possible only because of the mobility conferred by the horse.

The level of competitive riding in Britain between the World Wars was minimal in comparison with our present levels. Showjumping was in its infancy and the disciplines of eventing and dressage were virtually unknown. The British horse scene was based firmly on the hunting field, but in the summer months, if we are to believe the evidence of the equestrian magazines, hacking expeditions and DIY holidays on horseback were popular pastimes. Every issue of *Riding*, for example, then the leading, indeed, the sole horse monthly, contained, during the summer, accounts of rides in the West Country, through Wales and the New Forest, in Scotland and the Borders and, significantly, on bridleways all over the Home Counties. During the winter there would be articles on rides undertaken in faraway and often exotic places. Reading those issues now is to go back into a quieter, gentler world, retaining still an element of amateurism, and innocence too. A world in which, perhaps, the simpler, home-made pleasures were more appreciated. That at any rate is the retrospective view, but perhaps it was not really like that.

It was, of course, the time in which some of the most adventurous long-distance rides were made. In 1938, just before the outbreak of World War II, a young English girl taking a little money and a minimum of equipment rode right across Canada from Vancouver to Montreal (about 3,000 miles) then on to New York. Mary Bosanquet described her experiences in her book *Canada Ride*. It has to be the most casual epic ride that was ever undertaken.

Nothing, of course, can approach the ride of Aimé Tschiffely who with two Criollo horses, Mancha and Gato, made the 10,000-mile journey from Buenos Aires to Washington D.C. Starting in 1925 the ride took two and a half years. Tschiffely's book *The Tale of Two Horses* remains to this day a classic of its kind. Some 20-odd

The attractive rolling moorland of Dartmoor belies the presence of its deadly bogs.
(Picture courtesy of Drywells Farm)

years later Tschiffely wrote another, less well-known, book about a less adventurous journey. He called it *Bridle Paths* and it was about his 'leisurely jaunt' through England on horse-back. The idea, he said, was to 'jog along, anyhow and anywhere, canter, along quiet country lanes, over hills and through dales – sunshine or rain – alone with a horse to see the real England.' (Another 20 years on and the broadcaster Wynford Vaughan Thomas made a TV programme of a ride from one end of Wales to the other using the drove roads and the upland ways ridden once by the shadowy and usually tragic princes of Wales. Alas, as Wynford himself lamented, many of those historic routes are now closed to riders.)

In the same adventuring spirit are the much more recent rides made by Rosie Swale (*Back to Cape Horn*) and Robert Hanbury-Tenison (*A Ride Along the Great Wall*). In 1983 Rosie Swale rode 3,000 miles down the length of Chile, finishing in the biting winds, the snow and ice of Tierra del Fuego. Hanbury-Tenison, with his wife Luella, having ridden from Cornwall to the Camargue in 1984, took a couple of Chinese ponies along the Great Wall of China from end to end, all the way from the Yellow Sea to the Gobi Desert, a matter of 1,000 miles or so. Most recently Tim Severin rode to Jerusalem from Belgium, part of the way on an Ardennes Heavy

Horse, in the path of the First Crusade. Each journey was in the best tradition of the long-distance ride and demonstrated the elemental appeal of shared achievement – shared, that is, with the most adaptable and co-operative of animals.

The tradition of the DIY riding holiday persisted well after the end of World War II, when riding was becoming increasingly competitive, and it is not that much diminished today. It was reflected again in the magazines of the period, now much more numerous. In almost every issue of *Riding* during 1969 there were articles on rides taken in Britain and abroad. One, for instance, described a *trek* (the word had by then come into general use) of 200 miles along the Ridgeway, through Berkshire and Wiltshire, across Salisbury Plain into Dorset and then, via the New Forest, back to Surrey.

This sort of holiday was encouraged by the growth of a horse holiday industry, centred initially in the West Country and Wales but most particularly in Scotland, which may claim to have invented *trekking*, a major factor in the encouragement of Higland pony breeding. The word *trekking* (i.e. going from place to place) is of Dutch origin and, it is claimed, was brought back from the South African (Boer) War by Scotland's Lovat Scouts. Horse holidays remain with us and trekking establishments, catering for novice riders right through to the experienced horsemen, are to be found in every holiday area.

Central to the riding holiday whether organized or otherwise is the existence of rights of way on which horses can be ridden away from the dangers of slippery roadways carrying volumes of fast-moving traffic. The long-distance bridleways selected for inclusion in this book offer miles of just such riding through the rural heart of Britain, although some of them present challenges quite as great as the rides of yesteryear and none excludes the sense and something of the spirit of adventure.

Riders and ramblers sharing rights of way around the rugged Ramshaw Rocks in Derbyshire's Peak District.
(Picture courtesy of Northfield Farm / Amalia Pellegrini)

Bridleways

From the time that the Romans left Britain up to the making of the often much resented toll roads of the eighteenth century no main public roads were built. The countryside was criss-crossed with tracks, some dating from prehistoric times, and some relics of the Roman occupation. They were used for trade of all kinds – the transportation of wool and salt, both immensely important substances; lead, tin and coal from the mines and every other sort of commodity, all, of course, carried on pack-horses. Trains of 20 or more Dales and Fell ponies, for instance, carried heavy loads of lead (about 224 lb per pony) over the Pennines to Tyneside averaging as much as 240 miles a week over the difficult, narrow, yet clearly defined paths crossing the high uplands, parts of which are incorporated in the remarkable Pennine Way pioneered by Mrs Mary Towneley. The modern Cleveland Bay derived from the Chapman horses, the pack-horses of the travelling salesmen of north-east Yorkshire almost since medieval times. The Cleveland Way traverses much of the country crossed by the Chapmen.

Silbury Hill near the start of the Ridgeway. Nobody knows why or when it was built.

Well into the seventeenth century an established pack-horse service, using the now extinct Devonshire pack-horse, a steady trotting cob sort, was running between Brompton, Devon, and London. Some of that route survives in the Ridgeway detailed in the following bridleways section. Much later than that ponies were operating pack-trails in North Wales to carry slate from the quarries of Snowdonia to the ports of Bangor and Porthmadog. They would have used parts of the historic Pilgrims' Ride over which the devout made the pilgrimage to Bardsey, the island of the Saints, which lies just off the point at Aberdaron. This route and Glyndŵr's Way, which leads over some of the grandest and most rugged country in the north of Wales, were used, at least in part, by the preachers of the Methodist revival as they rode in every sort of weather from one isolated hill chapel to the other. The intrepid Mrs Daphne Tilley, who was instrumental in opening up and riding these paths, is indeed the descendant of a famous nineteenth century Welsh preacher who rode these paths extensively in the course of his ministry.

From ancient times there was this network of interconnecting paths and trails for local usage as well as for longer journeys. Furthermore, there was also a comprehensive and important system of long-distance drove roads, the equivalent of the modern trunk road system, which serviced the main centres of population and extended over the greater part of Britain. Many of the drove roads were still in use right up to the end of the nineteenth century. Over them thousands and thousands of cattle, sheep, pigs, geese and turkeys were driven. The drovers, particularly the cattle drovers who were the aristocrats of the trade, men of substance and well-respected, usually rode the ponies and cobs of their country, the Scots using sturdy Galloways, the mounts of the old border raiders, whilst the Welsh drovers whose numerous routes crossed the high, wild backbone of Wales used the cobs which were then integral to Welsh life, the descendants of those Powys cobs which from the twelfth century onwards had been the principal remounts of the English armies. Like the horses, the drover's cattle were shod for the journey to prevent them becoming lame, and even geese had their webbed feet protected by a pad of tar mixed with sawdust and grit.

All these 'rights of way' form the basis for the public paths which remain to us today. Obviously, the network of age-old tracks has been eroded over the centuries. The land enclosures of the eighteenth and nineteenth centuries caused the disappearance of all kinds of public routes and there was no one body to challenge the legality of the actions of many landowners. Railways, canals and roadways, built to service Britain's burgeoning industrial rôle, made further inroads into the public's right of access. Thereafter the speed of urban building and the intensification of farming practice all contributed to a diminishing number of public paths.

Nonetheless, no more than 70 years ago, when horses were still in general use and motor-cars were by modern standards comparatively scarce, traditional public

Snowdon provides the backdrop for riders on Moel Smytho near the proposed Pilgrim's Ride.
(Picture courtesy of Snowdonia Riding Stables.)

paths, whether for pedestrians or horsemen, were within reason commonplace enough and reasonably adequate for the national requirement of the day. In the years between the Wars it was possible, as the evidence of all those magazine articles shows, to ride quite extensively through rural England.

Increased leisure and affluence in the post-World War II years certainly put additional pressure on the means of public access to the countryside, but the needs of the war years also played a considerable part in the loss of time-honoured rights of way. Military camps, aerodromes, the increase in motorized traffic and the urgent need to produce more food for the beleagured nation all took their toll. Paths were closed by Emergency Orders, ploughed up, taken into existing fields, wired off and obstructed in all sorts of ways. The face of Britain was transformed within a decade and without public protest. The situation continued until after the War and it was only in 1949 that people and government began, belatedly, to appreciate the extent of their loss. As a result we had the National Parks and Access to the Countryside Act of 1949 which, amongst other things, required County Councils to produce, via Parish Councils, 'Definitive Maps' showing the position and type of rights of way within their areas, the emphasis being on the right of public usage. Some local authorities addressed themselves diligently to the problem, others were dilatory in their approach and the succession of subsequent, amending acts often delayed matters still further. By the time the Wildlife and Countryside Act of 1981 came into force, over 30 years after the Act of 1949, some counties had still to produce a complete Definitive Map, whilst the re-organisation of local government in 1974 caused more delay and not a little confusion.

Even today, the battle to maintain public rights of way continues. As recently as September 1989 the Countryside Commission published a paper under the title *Managing the Rights of Way Network: An Agenda for Action*. In it the Commission claimed that, of the existing 140,000 miles of rights of way in Britain 18 per cent were either impassable or in some way obstructed. The Commission laid the blame fairly and squarely on farmers for ignoring government guidelines and local authorities for failing to spend sufficient money on maintaining the paths and upholding the right of public access. The survey called for the 103 local highways authorities in England and Wales to spend between £14 and £21 million more per year to maintain the rights of way network.

Under the 1949 Act the Councils were required to list the ways under three headings: *Road Used as a Public Path* (RUPP, later changed to Byway), routes that might once have been used by vehicular traffic but were presently used largely for walking or riding; *Bridleways* and *Footpaths*. *RUPP*s were open to pedestrians and horses, whether ridden or led, possibly to vehicles and certainly to cycles. *Bridleways* were open to horse traffic and walkers and to cyclists who must give way to riders and pedestrians. *Footpaths* were reserved exclusively for the use of the latter.

Local authorities are bound by law to keep copies of the Definitive Map and to hold them available for inspection by the public. However, there is no guarantee, for a number of reasons, that the Ordnance Survey maps, on which the general public relies, will be entirely accurate in relation to the Definitive Map. Nor is there any guarantee that minor bridleways, although marked on the Definitive Map, will afford an entirely clear passage. If they are not used regularly, as the Countryside Commission's survey makes clear, they may have become overgrown or have been obstructed by the landowner's cultivation programme or even by the deliberate locking of gates. Where this is so the best course for riders to take is to report the matter to the local BHS Bridleways Officer who will have local knowledge and know what action to take with the local authority which is responsible for the upkeep of the path and for safeguarding its free access.

The advantage of riding the long-distance bridleways included in this book is that they are by and large fully established and the likelihood of obstruction is relatively small. In fact, the law regarding obstructions on rights of way is clear, the interpretation of obstruction wide, and the law very much in favour of the user. An obstruction, for instance, does not necessarily have to be a physical barrier, the interpretation extending as far as vocal abuse or intimidation. It is accepted that gates on a bridleway should be capable of being opened from the back of the horse. Indeed, should the gate be locked, and the path therefore obstructed in law, it is within the user's right either to go round, leaving the path if this is possible, or to remove the lock so as to be able to 'pass and repass' on the right of way. What must not be done is to go out with the specific intent to remove the lock – it can only be removed in passage as it were.

Much still remains to be done before today's riders can emulate Tschiffely's 'leisurely jaunt' through 'the real England' (or Scotland or Wales) but there are positive signs of progress. The existence of the long-distance bridleways which are the subject of this book are in themselves evidence of a rapidly changing climate of opinion and also of a growing determination on the part of individuals and groups to insist upon their rights of legal access.

The Countryside Commission is a growing force within the environmental lobby pressing for access to the country, whilst the farming community, faced with a new style of agricultural economy and the need, in consequence, to diversify, is becoming more sensitive about its public image in terms of conservation and of access, too. The Commission, which publishes a Code of Practice for farmers on the ploughing of public paths, as well as one directed to horse-owners and riders, is now proposing to provide at least one new long-distance bridleway during the next five years with more to follow.

Just as prominent is the British Horse Society's Access and Rights of Way Committee which co-ordinates the work of over 100 honorary Bridleways Officers throughout the the country. The Society's *National Strategy for Access* lays out the objectives for the next ten years. Principal amongst them is 'an established basic network of public bridleways and byways in all counties, with cross-country and regional links'. It also wants to see 'long-distance bridleways in most areas, linking so that a rider may travel the country if he so desires'. That final phrase may be seen as the consummation of the long-distance rider's ideal.

But if local authorities and landowners have obligations, so, too, do riders. If there is to be harmony there must be consideration for the needs of the countryside and of the people who make their living there. Gates which are opened must be shut to prevent valuable livestock from straying, horses ridden on the bridleway and not on adjoining land, and the enjoyment of walkers and cyclists respected. It is not considerate to do other than walk quietly past livestock. Galloping horses excite cattle, sheep and other horses unnecessarily and sometimes with serious consequences. Above all the Country Code has to be observed in all its aspects, particularly perhaps in respect of rubbish and damage caused to fences, trees and plants.

Most of us presume that the origin of the word bridleway rests on the word bridle and its connotation with horses and riding. The OED defines bridleway as 'a path fit for the passage of a horse . . .' but gives no clue as to when the word came into use.

Brecon Beacons. The view from the summit of the Sugarloaf. (David Ward.)

There is, however, a theory advanced that the original word was *bridalway*, the title given to the paths cleared beforehand for the royal progress made through his Kingdom by Henry VII and his bride Elizabeth of York. It is, one supposes, just possible, but if not it has at least the virtue of being a nice thought.

This is the Country Code which is applicable to all users of ways in the countryside:

1. Enjoy the countryside and respect its life and work.
2. Guard against all risk of fire.
3. Fasten all gates.
4. Keep dogs under close control.
5. Keep to the public path across farmland.
6. Use gates and stiles to cross fences, hedges and walls.
7. Leave livestock, crops and machinery alone.
8. Take your litter home.
9. Help to keep all water clean.
10. Protect wildlife, plants and trees.
11. Take special care of country roads.
12. Make no unnecessary noise. (If you must 'ride forth singing' do so *pianissimo* – the change to *fortissimo* can be made on uninhabited moorland etc.)

Preparation

Reconnaissance. The very essence of a successful long-distance ride is concerned with preparation and reconnaissance, so far as the latter is possible. The riding routes which follow are the best in the country and their rideability has been checked, but it is still necessary to plan the trip carefully.

1. *Select the route*, having regard for the time available, the distance and the nature of the ground to be covered, the existence of overnight stops and the severity of the ride in relation to the fitness of horse and rider. Unless the object is to compete against the clock, reckon upon covering 5–6 miles in the hour and riding between 12–25 miles per day. Some of the rides listed, or parts of them, are severe in terms of terrain and would not be suitable for other than experienced horse-people.

2. *Book accommodation along the route.* A good source of information is the BHS booklet, *Bed and Breakfast for Horses.* Make sure, however, of the facilities available. Riders will require an evening meal and horses will need stabling or grazing, concentrate feeds and hay. The BHS also publishes *Where to Ride*, a substantial country-wide guide-book which lists BHS approved riding establishments. These may be able to supply stabling, feed etc.

3. *Organize feed supplies.* If horse feed cannot be supplied at the overnight halts it will be necessary to convey foodstuffs to the halts in advance of arrival.

4. *Obtain a list of farriers and vets* within reach of the projected route. Normally, the people at the overnight stops will be able to help. Otherwise consult the most informative of annual equestrian publications, the *British Equestrian Directory*, obtainable from EMC, Wothersome Grange, Bramham, Nr Wetherby, West Yorkshire, LS23 6LY. This publication also lists riding schools, livery yards, studs, feed merchants, as well as taxidermists and tailors and most other things!

5. *Consider BHS membership* if you are not already a member. The advantages are very great. Over and above the contacts with local BHS officials of the regional or county organisation there is automatic third party insurance (public liability) against damage (or even death) caused by your horse.

6. Finally, *do some homework.* Read up all you can about the chosen route and the history of the area. Read, too, about the plants and trees you may expect to see, and also about the bird and animal life. Such knowledge adds greatly to the enjoyment of the ride. It is, indeed, surprising how much more can be seen from the back of the

There is no law of trespass in Scotland, but it is advisable to contact landowners.

horse. Animals and birds seem to accept a horse's presence when they would be startled by pedestrians or cyclists.

Clothes. The best advice is to travel light, a matter which will be appreciated by your horse. When Wynford Vaughan Thomas was planning his ride through Wales he sought the advice of a village tailor (now, one supposes, a breed extinct). 'Strong trousers,' he was told. 'With plenty of room in them.' That was good advice. Less satisfactory was the suggestion that for warmth he should wear a pair of ladies' tights under the generously cut nether garments. They were, said Wynford: 'Disastrous – hot, clinging, uncomfortable and quite unsuited for the male conformation!'

Tight clothes are not to be encouraged, whether outer garments or underwear. The latter, for all the modern developments, is best made from cotton, and a tee-shirt of the same material, under a good wool sweater, absorbs perspiration and acts to insulate the body.

Leather riding boots are smart and practical for most purposes but are not best suited for the business of riding miles over bridleways. They cause the feet to become hot, they can be difficult to get on and off and no good will be done to them if it is necessary to walk muddy or boggy ground. Lightweight chaps, worn over comfortable trousers and with strong, waterproof footwear are probably as good an arrangement as any.

However, if breeches or jodhpurs are preferred, let them be well-worn and comfortable – breeches cut like ballet tights are not comfortable. Most modern riding wear is made from man-made materials. That is all very well as long as one does not wear them for long distances in conjunction with synthetic saddles, rather than those made from conventional materials. The combination has the effect of overheating the lower regions most uncomfortably.

Absolutely essential is light waterproof gear which can be easily rolled and carried fastened to the forward dees of the saddle. The long, Australian pattern waxed waterproofs give overall protection to the rider as well as some cover to the horse. They are, moreover, very light in weight.

A hard hat, with a three-point fastening, conforming to British Safety Standards, is by any reckoning an obligatory piece of equipment.

If there is any likelihood of riding on roadways in the dust or after dark reflective clothing of some type is a necessity also.

A minimum of spare clothes can be carried. A change of underwear, for instance, slippers or something similar for the end of the day and perhaps a spare shirt.

Correct clothing for conditions, such as these on Exmoor, is vital. (John Watts)

Equipment. A plain snaffle *bridle*, without a noseband, which is then fitted over a *headcollar* is a practical piece of equipment. When making the midday halt the bridle can be removed to allow grazing and drinking. The headcollar needs to be fitted with a rope and an extra length of rope can also be carried along with pieces of twine. It should be possible to allow steady horses to graze if the rope, attached to a twine loop, is secured to something solid. (Temporary repairs can, of course, be made with short lengths of twine.) Do, however, make sure that horses are accustomed to the practice before setting out. Some people recommend fitting hobbles to the horse or tying to a proper tethering stake. Both are obviously effective but, once more, only if the horse has been trained to accept these methods. Of course, both are extra items which have to be carried.

Obviously, the *saddle* and its fittings are critical. Many long-distance riders in the more severe competitive rides use a Western saddle over a thick, folded blanket and there is much to be said for this arrangement. The Western saddle is heavy, of course, but allows the weight to be distributed over the largest possible bearing surface. Furthermore it was designed for long hours of riding and for much longer distances than the average British pleasure rider would contemplate.

There are, of course, saddles made especially for trekking or distance riding. Most of them are built on the principle of spreading the weight and not a few are based on the military trooper's saddle with 'fans' projecting behind the cantle. However, a well-fitting, general purpose hunting-type saddle which has plenty of dees for the attachment of bits and pieces and is neither too exaggerated in the dip of the seat nor in the forward cut of the flap and panel should be quite satisfactory for the distances involved in the present context. After all, a saddle which gives no trouble in a day's hunting, when one might expect to cover considerably more than 25 miles, is not going to create problems over that distance, much less a shorter one, when the horse is being ridden at a generally steady pace.

A reversible, easily washed and dried, *numnah*, foam-filled or something similar, will not come amiss. And, of course, one will need a pair of *saddle-bags* in which to stow one's gear. The design of this last piece of equipment has improved immeasurably in recent years as trekking has become popular. There should be no difficulty in obtaining roomy saddle-bags which lie in place without bumping about uncontrollably when the horse gets out of a walk.

A basic *grooming kit*, comprising no more than the bare essentials: brush, curry comb, sponges and a good, strong hoofpick is all that will be needed, but it is advisable to carry a second, folding hoofpick for emergencies.

Thereafter, one needs *maps* and a *map-case* with a plastic, rain-proof cover; a *compass* and possibly a small, wheeled *distance measurer*, a good *penknife* and, just in case, a pair of *wire-cutters*. The final items to be stowed in the saddle-bag are a light *hammer* with a claw head, a *farrier's buffer* and a pair of light *pincers*. These are extras, certainly, but they are invaluable if a shoe becomes lose or if it needs to be removed.

Room needs to be left for the human requirement – sandwiches, a bar of chocolate and a small carton of fruit juice. Wrapping paper and the empty carton are returned to the saddle-bag for later disposal: they are not left as litter!

A small plastic bottle of wound powder takes up no room, but a can of fly repellent is not as conveniently sized or shaped. It may be possible, however, to take small quantities.

Finally, take a whistle. If one is lost in a fog, for instance, whistle blasts blown at regular intervals may just produce some local help.

The Horse. Any sound horse of any type that is regularly ridden and is kept in good condition will have no trouble in doing 12 miles a day or even 20–25 at a steady pace. Most hunters, for instance, are exercised for 1½–2 hours per day and may expect to cover 10–12 miles at that time. 20 miles with an hour's rest given at midday is not excessive although it would be advisable to allow for a rest day or days if the ride was of a week's duration or more.

The most successful distance horses are Arabs, either pure- or part-bred but that does not preclude other breeds and types in rides of this nature. Temperament is, however, important. Highly strung, very nervous horses who may be unpredictable in their behaviour are not the best mounts on which to enjoy the beauty of the countryside – on the other hand it is quite extraordinary how sensible they become after a couple of days of steady work.

Horses will, of course, need to be fed adequately and regularly. The day should start with a good feed of nuts, mix or whatever the animal is usually fed and then time (about one hour) should be allowed for digestion before setting out. Horses can be allowed to graze at the halfway halt and every opportunity should be taken to offer them water. On arrival at the overnight halt another good feed can be given, after being made comfortable, and later the horse can have a substantial haynet.

It is sufficient if the horse is brushed over in the morning and made tidy. At the same time the feet can be picked out and the shoes checked for wear, security, risen clenches etc. In the evening, after a careful check for wounds, scratches, loose shoes etc, a quick brush to remove mud and sweat marks is sufficient. Whether horses are turned out at overnight stops or stabled is a matter of preference and may also depend on the facilities available.

Shoes. Horses should be shod three or four days before the journey to allow the shoe to settle to the foot and to ensure that they are entirely comfortable. Risen clenches, which may cause injury to the opposite leg, loose shoes etc can be dealt with on a temporary repair basis as long as the tools mentioned are carried. Thereafter, of course, the attention of the farrier must be sought.

Left: Snowdonia, like almost all the National Parks, offers exhilarating riding and scenery.

Dartmoor ponies. (John Heseltine.)

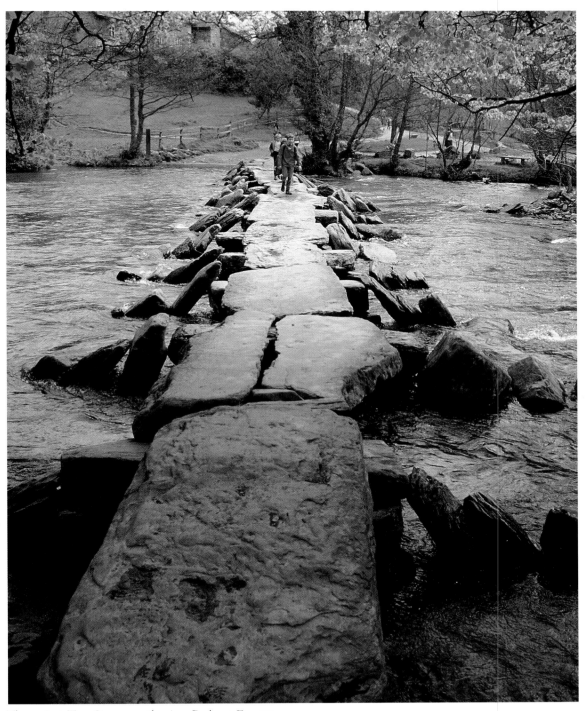

The ancient Tarr Steps cross the river Barle on Exmoor.

A shoe can be tightened by placing the buffer under the risen clench and tapping the blunt edge upwards with the hammer so that the clench lies straight up the wall. If there is a long end to the nail it can be twisted off with the hammer claw. Most of the operation to this point can be done by putting the foot on some improvised rest – a large stone will do well – but thereafter it is necessary to take the foot between the knees in the time-honoured fashion. Holding the foot in that way the head of the pincers is placed firmly under the clench, pressing towards the shoe, and the nail-head is tapped in. Reverting to the rest, the head of the pincers is then placed up against the nail-head and the clench hammered downwards and against the wall. Anything more than tapping with the hammer will be counter-productive.

If the shoe is beyond tightening and has to be removed, first cut off the clenches as before so that no resistance will be met when the shoe is pulled off the foot. Attempting to remove the shoe without taking this precaution will only result in the foot being broken. The shoe then has to be raised at the heels with the pincers and pressed down so that the nails are left projecting from the shoe. They can then be drawn out quite easily, but the pull must be a straight one and care must be taken not to break the nail by using too much force. In the same way the nails are taken from the quarters and then from the toe, when the shoe will come away without any possibility of the horn being broken.

Map-reading. A map is an essential piece of equipment. If you take the trouble to learn how to read a map it gives a very complete, birds-eye view of the countryside. It allows you to pinpoint your position and it tells you a great deal about the trail in front. In Britain, as in no other part of the world, we are fortunate that the whole of our country is mapped accurately and in great detail. The first one-inch map, in fact, covered the county of Kent and was published in 1801 and was extended over the next 70 years to cover the whole country.

Maps are made in a variety of scales. The clearest, as far as rights of way are concerned and the one most suitable for walkers, is the Ordnance Survey 1:25,000 series, but since each map covers only a limited area they are impractical for riders because of the disproportionate number that would be needed to cover a ride of even 50 miles. The scale most generally used is OS 1:50,000, which at 1¼ ins to the mile is much clearer than the old one inch to the mile map and more convenient than the 1:25,000. It has the additional advantage that it will continue to be a suitable scale (2cm to 1km) when, one supposes inevitably, the metric system is adopted.

The astonishing amount of information incorporated on a single OS sheet is almost as much as could be obtained from a fair sized book. A lot of it is given in the form of symbols printed on the right hand panel of the map. There are symbols for roads and paths; public rights of way; features, like quarries, woodlands, churches, with towers and spires, and chapels without either; and so as to cater for all the human need there is as well a list of abbreviations which includes the signs for a public house, a post office, a telephone box and a public convenience.

Bridges, railways, streams and rivers are all marked with appropriate symbols and, very importantly, the map is printed with contour lines, imaginary lines linking points of equal height which overcome the problem of depicting mountains, hills and changes in gradient. The height of the points is printed on the contour line and *the closer the contour lines are to each other the steeper is the gradient.* Black arrowheads on roadways are an additional aid to discovering steep gradients and always appear pointing downhill.

The ability to read the contours correctly makes it possible to gain a picture of the ground to be traversed, which may affect the timing of the journey. The other significant information revealed by a study of the contours is whether a particular feature is going to be visible from a specific point or whether it lies in a piece of dead ground, obscured by a ridge of spur, for instance. That is a most important factor in 'setting' the map in relation to the ground and, following that, establishing one's position.

Where am I? To find out it is necessary to identify features on the ground; a line of pylons, a road, a prominent hill or the ever-present and reassuring church, then find their corresponding symbols on the map. To 'set' or orientate the map with greater accuracy the north of the map has to point to the actual north on the ground. That is accomplished with a compass. Place the compass on the map, having made sure that there are no metallic objects in close proximity which would affect the reading, turn the map until the *magnetic north* (detailed in the symbol under 'North Point' is aligned to the compass needle. The precise position is then obtained by selecting two prominent features, one in the distance and one closer to, which are roughly in line. Identify the features on the map and draw a connecting line between them, extending it well beyond the nearest point. Next, line up two more features at right angles to the first ones and once more draw in a connecting line. Where the two intersect answers the question 'Where am I?'

Without a compass, North can be ascertained, in daylight, by using the sun and an ordinary wrist watch. The sun moves from east to west via the south and is due south at midday, a rough estimate of south and north can therefore be obtained using this knowledge. South (and north), however, can also be more exactly fixed by laying a watch in the hand and pointing its hour hand (don't bother about the minute hand) at the sun. *A line half-way between the hour hand and 12 o'clock points due south.* (Allowance can be made for the difference between G.M.T. and Summer Time for even greater accuracy but in practical terms it is hardly necessary.)

Map references. Precise positions of features etc, which may be necessary when arranging a rendezvous with a back-up team or other riders, are identified by a map or *grid reference.* Maps are divided into squares, ¾ ins apart on 1:50,000 sheets, the

Riding holidays from trekking centres are becoming increasingly popular such as this one on Dartmoor. (Picture courtesy of Drywells Farm)

horizontal and vertical lines being numbered. If, therefore, the point to be identified was a single church in one of these squares, the point is indicated by giving the pairs of horizontal and vertical numbers which coincide at the required square, i.e. 24/36. This is a four-figure reference, quite sufficient when the church is the only one in the square. A more accurate reference is made by imagining the square divided in ten by upright and transverse lines and using a six-figure reference i.e. 245/364. This is usually written '245364', as one number. The figure of the *vertical* line is always given first, working from the *bottom* of the map. The *aide-mémoire* is the phrase 'along the corridor and up the stairs'. To measure distances use a map measure calibrated to the scale of the map.

Riding Technique. Very simply, riding technique on a distance ride of the sort envisaged is governed by common sense. Give time to enjoy the scenery but when trotting for any distance be careful to ride some 5–10 yards ahead. That means, look out for alterations in the ground in front of you which could cause stumbling – ruts, very stony and rough surfaces – and always ride on the best surface available. When trotting, keep the speed down to a steady rhythm and rise to the pace. When cantering for short stretches, ease the horse in the same way by standing in the irons.

Take hills, whether going up or down, at a steady pace. Dismounting at very steep or rough descents is sensible and gives the rider a chance to stretch the legs. It is probably better to remain mounted when tackling a rise in the gradient, sitting well forward, giving the horse all the rein he needs and letting him take his own time. Getting off to walk up steep hills is exhausting for the rider and rarely satisfactory for either party.

It is unlikely that you will get lost, particularly if you have studied the route on the map and keep a lookout for prominent landmarks and features which are marked on it. If in doubt, stop and take time to consult and set the map. Checking positions from the moving platform of the saddle can be fraught with difficulties.

If you do get lost, the first and guiding rule is DON'T PANIC and don't split up if riding with companions. On open moorland, which can resemble a heather-covered desert without noticeable features, look for a stream and follow it downhill. It is bound to lead to roads, habitations or whatever. In woodland look for a path, however small. It will probably lead to a fence or a road eventually. Note carefully the position of the sun and the direction of the wind to prevent riding in circles. If ground becomes boggy, dismount and test it for yourself before proceeding. Heavy mists can come down quickly in high moorland country and it can be unnerving. Once more, do not panic. If it is really thick and the route ahead is unfamiliar, return to the ground you have already passed over and know.

The only helpful thing about fog is that sound travels more easily and if you stand still it may be possible to hear road noises or something similar. *In extremis* blowing a whistle may produce a result and, of course, the ability to use the compass will be a great source of comfort.

The horse's senses (including that of hearing) and his defensive instincts are very much more developed than ours. Left to his own devices a horse does not usually get stuck in bogs, for instance. Furthermore he has a far better sense of direction than we do. More often than not, if his rider drops the rein and lets him get on with it the horse will get himself, and his rider, out of trouble.

A sensible precaution and one always to be observed is to make sure that people at the overnight halts know from where you are coming and your approximate time of arrival and then know, also, where you are going on the following day and by what route.

Otherwise, 'go forth singing', if not with your voice then in your heart.

The South-West

Riders on Ley Hill above Porlock, overlooking the Bristol Channel. (John Watts.)

Dartmoor

The Dartmoor National Park is the largest open space in south-west England. Its open moorland, marked with granite tors, cut by valleys and streams, is a wild place of wheeling buzzards, blizzards in winter and fresh summer breezes. The landscape of peat and rock is high, often over 2,000 ft, and with 90 ins of rainfall a year always waterlogged. The beauty lies in the park's wilderness. However riding on the moor can be dangerous and should not be attempted by those who are strangers in the area. Even signposted bridleways can go through bogs so local knowledge is vital. There is no established long distance route on Dartmoor, although there have been proposals in the past. The Two Moors Way, from south-west to north-east across Dartmoor, then across Exmoor to Lynton, was abandoned as a route because of the dangerous roads it would have to cross. At the moment, North Devon's projected Tarka Trail is planned to extend south as far as the northern parts of Dartmoor, and parts of this trail are suitable for horses. As it is, riding on the open moors is generally allowed and is actually preferred by the National Park Authority to riding fixed routes because of the fear of erosion. Even the paths used by riding and trekking centres to gain access to the moor are often too heavily used. However, for those without local knowledge, the commercial riding stables are the only place to start.

The Dartmoor Commons Act of 1985 was passed to 'regularize', in the eyes of landowners and the National Parks Authority, the 'open access' of the moor for riders and walkers. Other national parks emphasize that land known as common is almost always owned by someone and traditional rights of access may be disputed. Another point to consider is that quite a lot of the northern half of the moor is used by the Ministry of Defence as a firing range from time to time so it is worth checking when.

Dartmoor is the eastern end of a long shelf of granite, connected underground, that runs from the Scilly Isles, through Lands End and Bodmin Moor. Added to this crystalline surface is the black peat, the purple, olive and white of the heather, and the rich green of the sphagnum moss. All around the moor proper, but still in the National Park, are pleasant green fields broken by hedges and spinneys of alder and birch. If you look closely at the plantlife on the tops, you will find the carnivorous sundew in the marshiest places, and in patches of bare peat left by hooves grows the pale butterwort. The birds you are likely to see include wheatears, skylarks, and around the woods, redstarts and wood warblers. There are red deer as well as roe and the introduced sika. Since the happy decline of the mink, the otter is returning, and may well strengthen in numbers as long as the animal rights people don't liberate any more fur farms. The otters live largely off the small brown trout, though the water board has kindly stocked its reservoirs with slow moving rainbow trout. There is a reasonable salmon run up the slightly acidic rivers of the northern moor, and at one or two waterfalls and bridges you can watch the fish leaping.

Like Exmoor the land is owned by many people and organizations, who take a hand in conservation. The Duchy of Cornwall has been one of the most important. The Prince of Wales owns about a third of the moor. The Duchy is responsible for many of the firebreaks through the heather, and has begun a scheme reintroducing the hardy

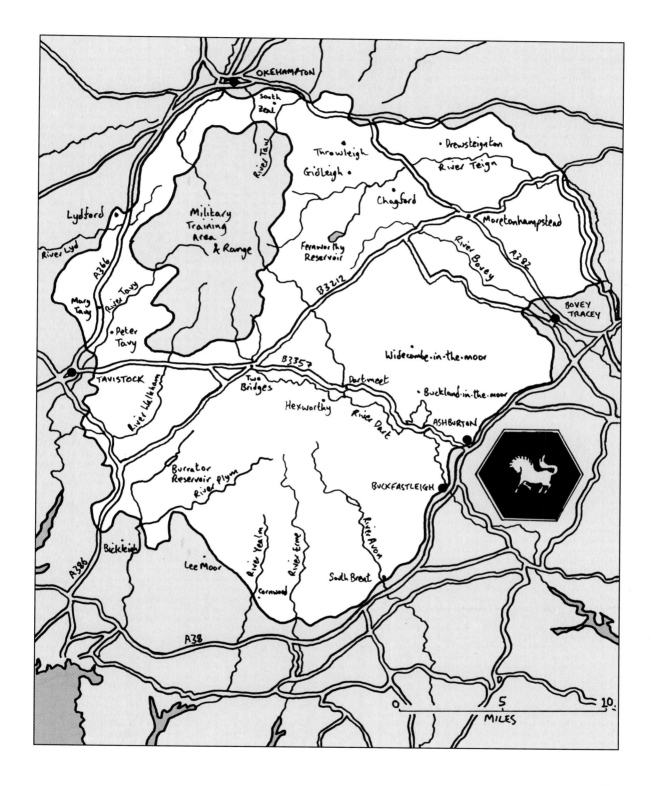

Dartmoor pony into some areas. The Dartmoor National Park Authority points out that it is an offence to feed these ponies, as that encourages them onto the roads. The Devon Wildlife Trust and the Dartmoor Preservation Association both work to keep the developers off the land, and preserve habitats. The berated Countryside Commission and the Nature Conservancy Council are government bodies which take a hand in keeping nature beautiful on Dartmoor. The National Trust, which owns Castle Drogo at Drewsteignton on the edge of the moor as well as over 5,000 acres is also actively involved in estate management and caring for the environment.

Okehampton is the most obvious starting point, because the main A30 road sweeps past it taking the tourists to the Cornish coastal resorts, and because the town has a good National Park information centre. It used to be a hellish place full of smog which built up in the Okement valley from the traffic driving through, but the bypass has changed all that. The town has risen and fallen many times since its Saxon origins, and nearly destroyed itself utterly during the Civil War. The Courtenay family, Earls of Devon, built the now ruined castle during the thirteenth century on the site of a Norman motte and bailey. When a later earl was executed, his estates passed into the hands of the crown.

Castle Drogo in Drewsteignton is a fascinating National Trust property. Having started his business life as a tea buyer in China, Julius Drewe was able to retire with a

A ride crosses the river Lyd on its return to Lydford House Riding Stables after an exhilarating hack over Dartmoor.

considerable fortune from his enterprise, the Home and Colonial Stores, at the age of 33. He then found a place in England which incorporated the name Drew and bought it. Castle Drogo was the house which Lutyens built for him above the village. It was started in 1911 and took nearly 20 years to complete. It is a vast building made of huge granite blocks overlooking the sheer Fingle Gorge. Everything about it is imposing, the oak bookshelves in the library, and even the cavernous kitchens. The roof leaks, it is cold, echoing and inhuman, and after Julius's death the Drewe family decided it was too much of a liability, and handed it over to the nation. Following the oak woods from Drewsteignton down the river you come to Fingle Bridge, a sixteenth-century, three-arched, granite bridge exploited as a beauty spot since the nineteenth century. On the 700 ft hill behind it is Prestonbury Castle, an Iron Age hillfort.

Chagford, in the other direction above the River Teign, has good views as far as Castle Drogo. Look out for the town's market house, which is known affectionately as the Pepperpot. Chagford was one of the first towns to realize the tourist potential of Dartmoor, and a local vicar made the place a 'headquarters for excursions'. In the porch of the Three Crowns, Sidney Godolphin, a poet, was shot during the Civil War, and he haunts the place to this day. Just above Chagford the North Teign river meets the South Teign to form the river Teign. The South Teign comes from Fernworthy Reservoir. Above the reservoir is the plantation Fernworthy Forest, and beyond that are two large circles of stones known as the Grey Wethers. There is another stone circle to the north, just west of Gidleigh, a village with part of a small Norman Castle. Moretonhampstead, known on the moor as Moreton, is a market town, once on the main

Ponies and black-faced sheep near Princetown.

Exeter to Bodmin road. It has some out-standing seventeenth-century granite alms-houses, as well as the site of an Iron Age hillfort nearby commanding the river Teign, called Cranbrook Castle. Grimspound, to the west of North Bovey, is the remains of a Bronze Age village.

The charming thatched granite cottages around the oak tree which stands on the green of Bovey Tracey mark the old western entrance to the moor. The church of St Peter, St Paul and St Thomas of Canterbury was founded by a local knight, Sir William de Tracey, who was repenting for his part in St Thomas's murder in 1370. It is a beautiful church with particularly good Beer stone arcades. The Manor House, now a hotel, was built in 1907 for Viscount Hambleden of W.H. Smith. Just outside the town is Parke, a farm in which rare breeds of sheep, poultry, old-fashioned pigs, and the especi-ally fine long-horned cattle are kept. The

miniature pony centre at Moretonhampstead is also worth visiting. The Becky Falls on a tributary off the Bovey, where that river plunges 70 ft off the moor, are most spectacu-lar after rain. Near them, to the west, is the precarious-looking Bowerman's Nose.

Widecombe-in-the-Moor is the scene for Widecombe Fair on the second Tuesday in September, famously attended by Old Uncle Tom Cobley and all. Rising out of the centre of the town is the 135 ft church tower, which is 24 ft longer than the church itself. The tower, which was added to the fourteenth-century church in the sixteenth century, earned it the name the Cathedral of the Moor. Widecombe is in a wide combe, a shallow valley, and Hameldown Beacon rises to 1,697 ft to the north-west. On the other side of that hill are a group of Bronze Age barrows. Buckland-in-the-Moor is noted for the face of the clock on its fifteenth-century church, which instead of

Riding on the Moor near Widecombe. (Picture courtesy of Drywells Farm.)

numbers is inscribed with the twelve letters MYDEARMOTHER. Dartmeet, to the west, is one of the most popular beauty spots with tourists. It is where the East Dart and the West Dart rivers meet. Holne Woods, between Buckland-in-the-Moor and Holne are also worth visiting.

The road between Tavistock and Ashburton was the old pack-horse route across the moor. Ashburton was first a centre for wool, but later became known for its slate quarries, which explains its slate-hung houses. It was also one of Devon's four stannery towns, along with Plympton, Tavistock and Chagford. During the Civil War number four North Street, then the Mermaid Inn, was one of Fairfax's headquarters. There are also some fine Regency villas to look out for. The town is dominated by the granite Perpendicular tower of its church.

Buckfast Abbey, just outside Buckfastleigh, was founded by Cistercian monks under King Canute. After the reformation it had nearly a 400-year break during which it fell into ruin. Monks fleeing France at the end of the nineteenth century came there and built their own abbey church, following the layout of the original, which was consecrated in 1932. It is a remarkable building of grey Limestone and Hamstone on the outside, and white Bathstone on the inside, most amazing because it was built entirely by the monks themselves, who had little knowledge of the necessary skills. At the centre, in Norman style, there is a crossing tower 158 ft high. It is now the home of the famous Catholic prep school. Buckfastleigh, to the south, which once depended on its wool and cloth,

Equestrian centre for moorland bridleways at Mary Tavy.
(J. C. Ticehurst.)

is now more widely acclaimed as the terminus of the Dart Valley Railway, the old GWR line which leaves the moor to follow the river Dart to Totnes. Between Ivybridge and Yelverton are three points of interest. Goodameavy is a pretty area of woods and moorland cut by a river: there is the extraordinarily shaped Dewerstone Rock; and there are the hut circles and good views from Wigford Down.

Dartmoor Prison at Princetown was built in 1808 by and for PoWs from the Napoleonic Wars. The land was donated by the Prince of Wales, later King George IV, thus the slightly colonial name of the local town, which is the largest and ugliest on the moor. Within a year it held some 9,000 men; and 2,000 Americans were added over the next four years for refusing to join the British navy against their home country. The place didn't become a convict prison until the 1840s when deportation ceased. Around Princetown are many hut circles and other prehistoric remains.

Two Bridges is the site of a hamlet which has grown up around this most important junction on the moor. Between it and the thirteenth-century clapper bridge, Postbridge, is Wistman's Wood with its extraordinary twisted dwarf oak trees, like a scene from a Van Gogh painting.

To begin with, Tavistock was a monastic borough. It gradually became important as a mining town, first for tin (it was named a stannary town in 1281), and then in the nineteenth century for copper; not to mention a profitable spin-off trade in refined arsenic, used extensively in dying processes at that time. Lead, iron, zinc and silver were also found in the area. In the nineteenth century the copper mine at Mary Tavy was one of the richest in the world. Just to the west is Brentor, which is crowned by the small stone church of St Michael's, built in the thirteenth century by a merchant fearful of a storm at sea, who wildly promised it to God as long as he escaped a watery death. He survived, though accepting bribes like that is likely to give God a bad name. Further up the River Tavy is the gorge the Tavy Cleave, and near it is a Bronze Age village on Standon Down.

Lydford, just inside the eastern border of the moor, has always been an important town. Its castle was built by the Saxons during the seventh century to ward off first the Celts and then the Danes. In 997 Lydford was sacked by the latter. The current ruins date from 1195, and were once a dungeon for prisoners awaiting trial. Lydford was a centre for tin mining, and the stanneries used to have their own courts. 'In the morn they hang and draw, and sit in judgement after', was said of 'Lydford Law'. Other points of interest include St Petroc's Church, which was probably founded by that Celtic missionary in the sixth century, and the sixteenth-century inn, which has on display a collection of coins minted in the village in the time of Ethelred the Unready (978–1050). Outside the village is Lydford Gorge, a steep cleft carved by the river Lyd, with a narrow 100 ft waterfall at one end.

OS Maps:190, 191.

Commercial Riding Centres:
Sarah Davies, Chagford Riding Centre, Waye Barton, Chagford, Devon TQ13 8DT, Tel: 0647 33519. Eastlake Stables, Belstone, Devon. Tel: 0837 52513. Elliott's Hill Riding Centre, Buckland-in-the-Moor, Devon. Tel: 0364 53058. Babeny Farm Riding Stables, Poundsgate, Devon. Tel: 0364 3296. Smallacombe Farm Riding Stables, Ilsington, Devon. Tel: 0364 6265. Mr A. & Mrs Diana Coaker, Great Sherberton Stables, Princetown, near Yelverton, Devon. Tel: 0364 3276. Mr R. E. Boulter, Lydford House Riding Stables, Lydford House Hotel, Lydford, Okehampton, Devon EX20 4AU. Tel: 0822 82347. Cholwell Farm and Riding Stables, Mary Tavy, near Tavistock, Devon. Tel: 0822 81526. Moorland Riding Stables, Moor Farm, Peter Tavy, near Mary Tavy, Devon. Tel: 0822 81293. Cheston Farm Equestrian Centre, Wrangaton, South Brent, Devon. Tel: 0364 73266. Lower Downstow Stables, Shipley Bridge Road, South Brent, Devon. Tel: 0364 73340. Mrs R. Hooley, Skaigh Stables Farm, Skaigh Garden Cottage, Belstone, Okehampton, Devon EX20 1RD. Tel: 0837 840429. Two Bridges Stables, Two Bridges Hotel, Princetown, Devon. Tel: 0822 89206. Aubrey and Margaret Hares, Blackslade Riding and Trekking Centre, Blackslade Farm, Widecombe-in-the-Moor, Newton Abbot, Devon PQ13 7TF. Tel: 0364 2304. Shilstone Rocks Riding and Trekking Centre, Widecombe-in-the-Moor, Devon. Tel: 0364 2281. Ruth Parnell, Drywell Riding Centre, Widecombe-in-the-Moor, Newton Abbot, Devon TQ13 7PN. Tel: 0364 3349. Mrs A. Howard, Crossways Riding School, Axtown Lane, Yelverton, Devon PL20 7EB. Tel: 0822 853025. Hillside Riding Centre, Merrivale, Yelverton, Devon. Tel: 0822 89458.

Accommodation with stables:
Mrs S. M. Forbes, Beardon Farm, Two Bridges, Yelverton, Devon PL20 6SR. Tel: Princetown 287. Mrs P. Powell, Cuming Farm, Colston Road, Buckfastleigh, Devon EX16 7RY. Tel: Bampton 31205. Mrs P. Richardson, Stoke Court, North Huish, South Brent, Devon. Tel: 0364 72523. Miss P. Neal, Middle Stoke Farm, Holne, Ashburton, Devon TQ13 7SS. Tel: Poundsgate 444. Mrs S. Meadows, Holystreet Manor, Chagford, Devon TQ13 8HQ. Tel: Chagford 3416. Mrs J. F. R. Weir, Parford, Chagford, Devon TQ13 9JR. Tel: Chagford 2221.

Vets
Claydon and Young. Tel: 0837 2148. N. J. Harrison, Hazeldene, Ashburton, Newton Abbot, Devon. Tel: 0364 52571.

Farriers:
Mark Andrew Svensson RSS, Church View, South Zeal, Okehampton, Devon EX20 2PS. Tel: Sticklepath 258. L. J. P. Middleton RSS AFCL, Moorview, Didworthy, South Brent, Devon TQ10 9EF. Tel: South Brent 3491.

Further Help:
Mrs J. Cox, British Horse Society County Bridleways Officer Devon, Preston, Drewsteignton, Exeter EX6 6PP. Tel: 0647 21231. Alison Cumberley, Dartmoor National Park Officer, Dartmoor National Park Office, Parke, Haytor Road, Bovey Tracey, Newton Abbot, Devon TQ13 9JQ. Tel: 0626 832093. Jo Chisholm, Long Distance Riding Group (Dartmoor), 50 Moorview, Hatherleigh, Okehampton, Devon EX20 3LB.

Exmoor

Unlike Dartmoor you are not encouraged to ride everywhere on Exmoor, and, because of the bogs, it is wise to ride with someone who has good local knowledge. The farmers have the last word on where horses can go, and some of them grant the curiously named 'permissive paths' across their land. But as an article in *The Exmoor Visitor* stated: 'A farmer's readiness to permit the lone walker to cross his land can quickly turn to reticence when his facility is used by the mass sponsored walk: or when the bridleway through his farmyard is used regularly by the pony trekking party.' Exmoor is hunted quite thoroughly, and when the horses and hounds cross fields in wet weather, or during lambing, farmers can suddenly become un-

sporting. The Park Authority here, as with Dartmoor, promotes riding through commercial stables and centres, so that overall management and relations with those involved is made easier.

Horses are taken extremely seriously on Exmoor. The moor is the venue for the great and gruelling Golden Horsehoe Ride, and there are enough interconnecting tracks to ensure that the route is different each year.

At a mere 265 square miles, Exmoor is one of the smallest of Britain's National Parks. The scenery consists of rolling peat moors among curious flat-topped hills. Due to the almost continual rain the going is soft on the hooves along the heather, but paths are interspersed with steep stony tracks. You and your animal can be any size, but you both need to be fit. Exmoor is rich in bird-life, from pipits to the larger birds of prey,

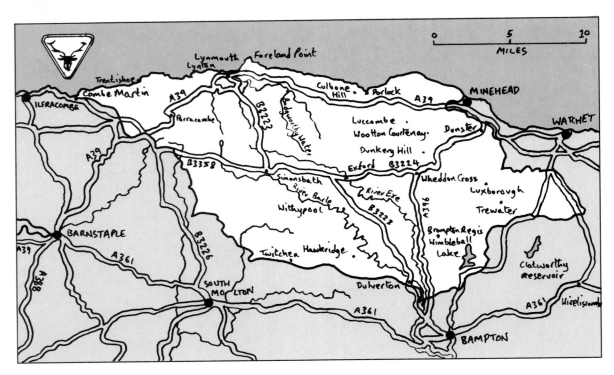

A tempting jump, but a trap for the unwary on Brendon Common.

Button Bridge Valley. (Picture courtesy of Arlington Riding Centre.)

indeed the whinchat is seldom seen outside the moor. The most obvious animals are the red deer and the Exmoor ponies. The deer are extremely wary of man, but are prolific and hunted by the Devon and Somerset Staghounds which are based in Exford. Other hunts on the moor include the East and West Dulverton Foxhounds, the Minehead Harriers and the Exmoor Foxhounds. The ponies have been hailed as the last direct descendants of the horse which survived the last Ice Age. The Park Authority has set up four pure herds, on East Anstey Common. Warren Farm, Haddon Hill and Larkbarrow. The Authority likes to stress that Exmoor is a place for living and working. The present priorities are conservation and management of resources to promote tourism, so more and more local people are turning away from traditional pursuits to the tourist industry for their income.

Until quite recent history this part of the country was all but cut off from the rest by the marshy and impassable Somerset Levels. It was the ancient British kingdom of Dumnonia, and was not invaded by the English until the seventh century. It is dotted with ancient remains, such as the stone circles on Withypool Hill and Porlock Common, and steeped in legend. One of the rocky outcrops on the north coast is Sir Robert's Chair, where centuries ago one Sir Robert Chichester was condemned to sit each year and weave sand into bridles and reins in order to drive a burning carriage up past Desolate Combe.

Combe Martin is the town which marks the western point of Exmoor. It is not a beautiful place, but has enjoyed a long and varied career. It used to be an important centre for silver mining, and some of the old shafts run under the streets. To enhance this shanty town feeling there is the Pack of Cards pub, which was built by a gambler, and looks like a house of cards. The church is fifteenth-century and has the only painted rood screen on Exmoor. East of Combe Martin, beyond Hangman's Hill is Watermouth Castle, which was built in 1825. If you ride east along the coast you will see the fine views from Trentishoe Down, and you can descend to Heddon's Mouth, which is a secluded cove at the bottom of high cliffs. To the south is Parracombe with the notable St Petrock's Church. Back on the coast again is Woody Bay and the extraordinary

Bridge over the river Avill, looking towards Dunster Deer Park. (John Heseltine.)

Valley of the Rocks, the dry gorge where the East Lyn river used to flow. Beyond it is Lynmouth.

Much of Lynmouth was swept away in 1952, when freak floods on Exmoor destroyed almost 100 houses and 28 bridges, killing 31 people. However, the harbour area survived, and it is surrounded by pretty thatched cottages. Lynmouth is a town trapped by its position. It could never grow any larger because of the steep hills directly behind it, and, in fact, the road to Countisbury climbs the Old Barrow Hill to over 1,000 ft above sea-level. The poet Shelley loved Lynmouth for its size and aspect, though, and stayed in the town in 1812. Lynton, which towers above Lynmouth at the top of a nearly sheer cliff, was built during the nineteenth century to take the overflow from Lynmouth, and a cable railway was added between them in 1890. It has now outgrown its parent town. At Countisbury there is a fourth-century Roman earthwork called the Signal Station. There are a number of points of interest in the vicinity. The 1952 flood disaster came through the Glen Lyn Gorge. It is now the spectacular site of a hydro-electric scheme with a permanent exhibition about the history of water power. The Natural History Centre in Malmshead is run by members of the Exmoor Natural History Society and has all the latest information about the National Park. The National Trust owns Watersmeet near Lynton, which is a beautiful wooded area where the East Lyn river and Hoaroak Water meet. Brendon is a pretty village on the East Lyn, with thatched, whitewashed cottages, and Foreland Point is most imposing. The area around the village of Oare was made

Porlock, at the foot of Bossington Point.
(J. C. Ticehurst.)

famous as the setting for Blackmoor's *Lorna Doone*. The Doones' house is attributed to the ruins in the abandoned village of Badgworthy, and Malmsmead Bridge in the Badgworthy Valley is worth seeing.

The inaccessible village of Culbone along the coast has the smallest church in Britain, St Beuno's, only 12 ft 4 ins wide, and a little under 34 ft long. According to legend the spire was confiscated from the church at Porlock by St Michael and presented to Culbone, whose citizens were obviously more in the Almighty's favour than those from Porlock. There was a colony of lepers nearby during the Middle Ages who were not allowed into the church, but were made to watch the services through a window. The farmhouse just above Culbone was where Coleridge was interrupted whilst writing *Kubla Khan* by a person on business from Porlock. Once again Porlock's history is blighted by greater events in Culbone. If you retrace that unhappy person's route home over the towering Porlock Hill you will come to Porlock itself, a large village with a variety of interest. There is a famous riding school, and to the east of St Dubricious's Church is the fifteenth-century manor, Doveray Court, which has been turned over to reading rooms. Between Porlock and Exford is Stoke Pero, which has the highest church on Exmoor. Nearby is the neolithic burial site Kit Barrows, and the cliffs of Hurlstone Point are magnificent.

Bossington is a pretty village, with walnut trees, and a sixteenth-century chapel attached to the old manor. Selworthy in the Vale of Porlock, with its odd white church, is a beautiful village of thatched cream cob cottages with a fifteenth-century tithe barn and an ancient earthwork called Bury Castle. Selworthy's tea shop recently won an award for the best cup of tea in the country! Selworthy Beacon is 1,013 ft above sea-level and the views from the top are outstanding. There are pack-horse bridges at Horner, West Luccombe and Allerford. The one at Horner is at the bottom of a delightful cleft of woodland, and the one at Allerford is high-arched and stands by a ford in the shade of walnut trees. There is a working water mill in Wootton Courtenay, which is

Beech hedges surround a bridleway at Brayford. (Picture courtesy of Arlington Riding Centre.)

The stables at Dunster Castle. (John Heseltine.)

A Golden Horseshoe contender at Piles Mill, Holnicote, a National Trust Property. (Glyn Satterley)

now a pottery with extremely fine pieces for sale, as well as the opportunity to watch the potter at work.

Just to the west of Minehead is North Hill with its neolithic barrows. Along the coast you might see the last sea-going paddle steamer in the world, the *Waverley*, and the cruise ship the *Balmoral* plying their way up and down the north Devon coast with parties of sightseers.

Another working watermill, this one in Dunster, produces stoneground whole-wheat flour, and has an adjoining museum. It is open on most days from April to October. The town of Dunster nestles in a valley between the Conygar Tower and Dunster Castle. It was first important as a port, but the river silted up during the middle ages. Dunster retrieved its fortunes and managed to grow with its trade in cloth. The eight-sided Yarn Market originally built in 1589 is worth looking at, the Butter Cross is medieval and the Gallox Bridge was built for packhorses. The town also has a Benedictine priory which became the largest church on Exmoor after the reformation, the Luttrell Arms Hotel which was one of the residences of the Abbots of Cleeve during the Middle Ages, and the Conygar Tower to the north built in 1775, which was a well-known landmark for sailors coming towards the Bristol Channel. Dunster Beach is a popular spot for holidaymakers, but by now you are not that far from Hinkley Point nuclear power station.

Only two families have owned Dunster Castle during its 900-year history, the Mohuns and the Luttrells. It was built soon after the Norman Conquest on the site of a mill mentioned in the Domesday Book and, in the manner of great castles everywhere, has had pieces lopped off and added on in the ensuing centuries. The fine gatehouse was built by Sir Hugh Luttrell in 1421. Croydon Hill lies to the south of Dunster Castle, and has been planted with soft woods. Although the hill is exposed, there are many sheltered tracks running through the wood crisscrossed with deer tracks. These make enjoyable rides with overwhelming views of Blue Anchor Bay to the east, and the rolling hills of the rest of the moor to the west.

In the Raleigh's Cross area you are on the edge of the Quantock Hills. Bill Poirrier is the blacksmith at Riverden Forge in Road-water. His showrooms contain items such as wrought iron candlesticks, decorative candles made by his wife Margit, and wool spun by their daughter Stella. Moving along, the Elizabethan house and gardens, Combe Sydenham Country Park, is in Monksilver. It is open from April to October every day except Saturdays.

After crossing the Brendon Hills you come to Dulverton, which has been the main town in this area of Exmoor since the thirteenth century. For this reason it is a curious hotch potch of architecture. The ruined Bar-linch Priory is nearby. In the seventeenth century, near Molland, just south of the moor, the two brothers James and Henry Quartly created the strain of cattle known as the Red Devon from the local breed. They also invented the hill farm irrigation method of channelling streams across hillsides. Further west is North Molton which was an important copper mining centre.

Until 1818 the whole area around Simons-bath was covered by a royal hunting forest, and the seventeenth-century Simonsbath House was built by James Boevey, who was one of the forest wardens. John Knight, who came from Worcestershire, bought the house and the forest, walled it off, and turned it into a profitable estate. It is now broken up, but vestiges of Knight's works

Badgworthy Water, site of the legendary Doone Valley.

such as the introduction of new breeds of livestock, and the building of Pinkworthy Road, are still apparent. In Simonsbath itself there is a monument to Sir John Fortescue, (1859–1933) who was the Librarian at Windsor Castle, and a noted historian. From this pretty village you can go to the Chains, which, at 1,599 ft, is the second highest point on Exmoor, and beyond it are the neolithic remains of the Chapman Barrows.

Exford is the heart of Exmoor, both geographically and spiritually. The Exmoor pony sales are held here. Tarr Steps to the south, near Hawkridge, is an ancient causeway over the river Barle, in the form of a stone 'clapper bridge' with unknown origins. After being washed away in the 1952 flood it had to be rebuilt, and was most recently restored in 1980. At Winsford Hill there is a stone, bearing the inscription *Carataci Nepus*, Kingsmen of Caratacus, who was a chieftain during the early years of the Roman occupation. Nearby Dunkery Beacon is the highest place on the moor at 1,705 ft above sea-level. From its top on a clear day some 14 counties can be seen, from Bodmin Moor to the Blackdown Hills, and to the Black Mountains of Wales.

OS Map: 180

Commercial Riding Centres:
D. T. Dascombe and Son, Burrowhayes Farm, West Luccombe, Porlock, Somerset. Tel: 0643 862463. N. H. Williams, Horner Farm Riding Stables, Horner, Porlock, Minehead, Somerset. Tel: 0643 862456. Mrs Marion Balman, Arlington Riding Centre, Tidicombe Farm, Arlington, near Barnstaple, Devon EX37 4SP. Tel: 0271 82300. Mr and Mrs N. Hutchings, Riscombe Farm, Exford, Minehead, Somerset TA24 7NH. Tel: 0643 83480. Mrs Helen Bingham, Outovercott Riding Stables, Barbrook, Lynton, Devon EX35 6JR. Tel: 0598 53341. Mr W. J. Burge & Miss N. Stafford, Doone Valley Riding Stables, Parsonage Farm, Oare Brendon, Lynton, Devon EX35 6NU. Tel: 0598 7234. Ken H. Pettit, Lower Dean Farm Hotel, Dean, near Parracombe, Devon. Tel: Parracombe 215. Mr and Mrs B. Wollacott, Brendon Manor Farm, Brendon, near Lynton, Devon. Tel: 0598 7546. Mrs R. I. Bullman, Pine Lodge Riding and Holidays,

Higher Chilcott Farm, Dulverton, Somerset. Tel: Dulverton 23559.

Accommodation with stables:
Wheel Farm Country Guest House, Berrydown, Combe Martin, Devon EX34 0NT. Tel: 0271 882550. Mrs J. Holton, East Bodley, Parracombe, Near Barnstaple, Devon EX31 4PR. Tel: 0598 3227. Mr David W. and Mrs Rose Dyer, The Silver Horse Shoe, High Bullen Farm, Barbrook, Lynton, Devon. Tel: 0598 53318. Mrs Butler, West Ilkerton Farm, Lynton, Devon EX35 6QA. Tel: Lynton 52310. Mrs K. Stevens, Cloutsham Farm, Porlock, Minehead, Somerset TA24 8JU. Tel: 0643 862839. Mrs T. Andrews, Woodcocks Ley Farm, Porlock, Somerset, TA24 8LX. Tel: 0643 862502. Mrs E. J. Richards, Silcombe Farm, Porlock, near Minehead, Somerset TA24 8JN. Tel: 0643 862248. Judy Robinson, The Ship Inn, High Street, Porlock, Somerset TA24 8QD. Tel: 0643 862507. Mr and Mrs A. J. Hill, The Old Manor, Lower Marsh, Dunster, Somerset TA24 6PJ. Tel: 0643 821216. J. Lamacraft,

Knowle Riding Centre.

Knowle Riding Centre, Timberscombe, Minehead, Somerset TA24 6TZ. Tel: 0643 84342. Roger and Penny Webber, Hindon Farm, near Minehead, Somerset TA24 8SH. Tel: 0643 5244. Mrs J. Haffner, Wanneroo Farm, Timberscombe, Somerset TA24 7TU. Tel: 0643 84493. Mrs S. Richmond, Hungerford Farm, Washford, Watchet, Somerset TA23 0LA. Tel: 0984 40285. Mrs E. V. Brown, Emmetts Grange, Simonsbath, Minehead, Somerset TA24 7LD. Tel: 0643 83282. Mrs Gillian Lamble, Edgcott House, Exford, near Minehead, Somerset TA24 7QG. Tel: 0643 83495. Exmoor Lodge, Exford, near Minehead, Somerset. Tel: 0643 83615. Mrs Celia Sharman-Courtney, Folly, Winsford Hill, Winsford, near Minehead, Somerset TA24 7JL. Tel: 0643 85253. Stockleigh Lodge, Exford, near Minehead, Somerset. Tel: 0643 83500. The Crown Hotel, Exford, Somerset TA24 7PP. Tel: 0643 83554/5. Sylvia and Ray Jenkins, Batsom Farm, Withypool, Somerset TA24 7RG. Tel: 0643 83541. Mr and Mrs D. R. Bacon, Holly Cottage, Ashlane, Winsford, Somerset TA24 7JH. Tel: 0643 85425. Mr and Mrs Cody-Boutcher, Little Quarme Country Holidays, Wheddon Cross, near Minehead, Somerset TA24 7EA. Tel: 0643 85249. Exton House Hotel, Exton, Dulverton, Somerset TA22 9JT. Tel: 0643 85365. Mr C. Steven, Royal Oak Inn, Winsford, near Minehead, Somerset TA24 7JE. Tel: 0643 85455. Mrs June Fisher, Rivendale, Huish Champflower, Taunton, Somerset TA4 2BX. Tel: 0984 23070. Tarr Steps Hotel, Hawkridge, Dulverton, Somerset. Tel: Winsford 0643 85293. Mr and Mrs Harper, The Froude Arms, East Anstey, Tiverton, Devon EX16 9JP Tel: 0398 4223. Mrs A. M. Spencer, Dassels Guest House, near Dulverton,

Somerset TA22 9RZ. Tel: 0398 4203. Mrs E. M. Hancox, Hinam Farm, Dulverton, Somerset TA22 9QQ. Tel: 0398 23405. Mr and Mrs P. Strong, Lower Chilcott Farmhouse, Dulverton, Somerset. Tel: 0398 23439. Mrs H. J. Milton, Partridge Arms Farm, West Anstey, South Molton, Devon. Tel: 0398 4217. Mrs F. Govier, Rainsbury Farm, Upton, Wiveliscombe, Somerset TA4 2HU. Tel: 0398 7241. Bridge House Hotel, 24 Luke Street, Bampton, Devon EX16 9NF. Tel: 0398 31298. The Courtyard, Bampton, Devon. Tel: 0398 31536. Lion Hotel, Bank Square, Dulverton, Somerset TA22 9BU. Tel: 0398 23444. Mr and Mrs J. Phripp, Anchor Inn, Exebridge, Devon. Tel: 0398 23433. Exeter Inn, Tiverton Road, Bampton, Devon EX16 9DY. Tel: 0398 31345. Ann Bevan, West Knowle House, Brushford, Dulverton, Somerset TA22 9RU. Tel: Dulverton 23835.

Vets:
West, Carter & Browne, White Lodge, Whitegate Road, Minehead, Somerset TA24 5SP. Tel: 0643 3649 or 0984 6289. Fuller, Thompson & Elliot, Duckpaddle, Dulverton, Somerset. Tel: 0398 23285.

Farriers:
John Kent RSS, The Forge, Exford, Minehead, Somerset. Tel: Exford 264. R. Veale RSS AFCL, Swincombe, Bishopsnympton, South Molton, Devon EX34 4PS. Tel: Bishopsnympton 310.

Further Help:
Mrs J. Conachie, British Horse Society, 5 Woodford Cottage, Woodford, Wilton, Somerset. Tel: 0984 40762. Dawn Metrevors, Exmoor National Park, Exmoor House, Dulverton, Somerset. Tel: 0398 23665.

The Wiltshire Droves

The Oxdrove and the Herepath. These are two ancient droves roads in the southern part of Wiltshire, making a good weekend ride. The Oxdrove bridleway runs between the A354 near Knighton Wood and Berwick St John, and the Herepath bridleway links Whitesheet Hill with Salisbury race-course, south of Wilton. They are used as part of a larger linked ride organised by the British Horse Society in April, and in turn that forms part of an even larger ride, The Three Rivers International Ride, which takes place in September. The general area of these rides is south and west of Wilton, the ancient capital of Wessex.

Wilton had, and still has, a famous market. The droves were originally routes to drive cattle between farms and markets or fairs, thus the name Oxdrove. They were most used from the seventeenth century, but declined with the coming of the railways. They tended to be broad and grassy, like herepaths. The word *herepath* was Anglo-Saxon for any road which wasn't Roman. A Roman road, which was usually known to the Anglo-Saxons for being at least partially paved, was called a *straet*. You occasionally come across a farm called Harepath, a corruption of this word.

Starting on the Herepath from Whitesheet Hill, on the A30, near Donhead St Andrew, you ride east and cross Cross Dyke. Unlike eastern parts of the Oxdrove, the Herepath is well waymarked. Gallows Hill is on the right, and the village of Ansty is over the A30 on the left. The ridge continues past Middle Down and then Swallowcliffe Down, beyond which is Swallowcliffe itself. Prescombe Down is on the right and Sutton Down on the left, then Fifield Down and Fovant Down. The giant regimental badges were cut into the chalk of Fovant Down by battalions stationed in the area in 1916. They include a couple of Australian regiments, as can be seen from the kangaroo and maps of Australia, as well as the badge of the RAMC, the 6th City of London Rifles, the YMCA triangle, the London Rifle Brigade, the 7th Royal Fusiliers, the deer of the Royal Warwickshire Regiment, and the castle of the Devon Regiment. This landmark and others like it were covered up during World War II to confuse enemy aircraft. The prehistoric remains at Chiselbury are a good viewing point.

As you ride on, Compton Down is on the left, and the village at its foot is Compton Chamberlayne. You go over Hydon Hill, and past the wood, Burcombe Ivers, which cascades down the side of the hill to the left. Hoopside, which is a continuation of that scarp, looks like the auditorium of some giant arena. Barford St Martin is directly beyond it over the River Nadder, and Burcombe is just downstream. The descent to the finish of Salisbury race-course is through the woods in Hare's Warren, where you will find the remains of Neale's Barrow.

Wiltshire is named after Wilton, which was the capital under King Ine of Wessex, towards the end of the seventh century. He used it as a base while gerrymandering the ancient 'hundreds' into counties. In those days it was little more than a fort. King Alfred founded a Benedictine convent there 200 years later, and evidence of 12 churches in the town has been discovered. However, another 200 years after that it was sacked by the Danes, and since then has never managed to keep up with the pace of growth of nearby Salisbury. The Gothic church at the end of the avenue of ruined arches was

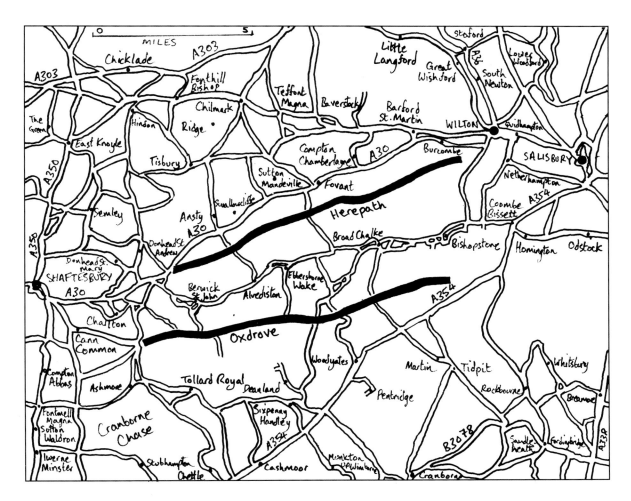

restored earlier this century by Robert Bingham, once United States Ambassador to
Britain. His ancestor, also Robert Bingham,
was consecrated bishop in the church in the
early thirteenth century. Wilton is known
for its carpets and the Royal Wilton Factory
is open to visitors. At one time, a pair of
Huguenot weavers were desperately required but were forbidden to leave France,
so the 8th Earl of Pembroke, who had an
interest in the factory, arranged for these
craftsmen to be smuggled into Britain in a
wine barrel.

Wilton House is one of the greatest of the
country houses. From being a convent before
the reformation, it was given to Henry VIII's
favourite William Herbert, who later became the 1st Earl of Pembroke. It has stayed
in the hands of the gregarious Herbert family
ever since, though the present Earl, who is a
film director, has opened it to the public. It
was first designed as a house fit to entertain
Edward VI. Under the 4th Earl a fire destroyed it, so a new building was put up,
designed by Inigo Jones and John Webb,
the architect's son-in-law. Members of the
Herbert family have always impressed their
characters on the place. The famous Palladian bridge was built under the 9th Earl,
and in 1801 the 11th Earl had most of the
house rebuilt by James Wyatt. The 2nd Earl
married the sister of the poet Sir Philip

The view from Swallowcliffe Down on the Herepath, towards Whitesheet Hill.

Sidney, and he wrote his famous work *Arcadia* at the house. Marlow, Ben Jonson and Edmund Spenser all visited, and there is some evidence that Shakespeare did too. It was a popular stop for Charles I, which was expensive. Other Herberts have been travellers, soldiers, leading experts on equitation, but above all patrons of the arts. The house is famous for Adam's magnificent white and gold Cube Room and Double Cube Room, which contain stunning portraits.

There is a link between the Oxdrove and the Herepath along a Roman road. They are similarly linked at the western end for the British Horse Society ride. In fact Wiltshire is covered with droves, 'trackways' and 'ridgeways', and many of them can be ridden. There is endless riding along paths and bridleways in Wiltshire which local groups have spent years discovering and gaining official recognition for. This Roman road goes through the pretty ford at Stratford Tony and past Bishopstone. If you stop in Bishopstone look out for its fine Decorated church, possibly by William of Edington, Bishop of Winchester at the end of the fourteenth century. The woodwork in the

pews and the pulpit is thought to be foreign, perhaps Spanish.

The Oxdrove runs parallel to the Herepath on the way back west but further south, starting from near Knighton Wood, south of Knighton Hill. Leaving Middleton Hill and Knowle Hill on the right you come to Vernditch Chase with its barrows and enclosure. Halfway along the west side of this wood is the point at which the three counties of Hampshire, Wiltshire and Dorset meet.

After Vernditch Chase you go past Marleycombe Hill on your right, with the earthworks on its summit, beyond which is Bowerchalke. From Cowdown Hill and Woodminton Down, you can look north over the valley of the river Ebble to the ridge which carries the Herepath. Stonedown Wood comes up on the metalled road, but the local landowners are most helpful as long as it is not harvest time. To the right is Alvediston, beyond South Down and Trow Down.

The beeches of Chase Woods on the left are largely what remain of the thick forest which used to cover Cranborne Chase. Cranborne Chase is an area of about 100 square miles, and was originally the hunting ground of the Dukes of Gloucester. Then King John took over those rights, which stayed in the hands of the royal family until James I. The Earls of Salisbury were the next to stock their ample larders with the indigenous fallow deer, and then the Earls of Shaftesbury. Finally the Pitt-Rivers family took it on, but by then it had become such a liability, with frequent pitched battles between keepers and poachers, that in 1830 Parliament stepped in. For a while it was a haven for smugglers and highwaymen. The building that houses Cranborne Chase girls' school was once owned by the Pitt-Rivers family. Incidentally, it was after he saw some of the young ladies from that school at Waterloo Station that Ronald Searle was inspired to write the *St Trinians* books.

As you continue Rotherley Down is on the left, between Rotherly Bottom and Malacombe Bottom, and beyond it is Tollard Royal. In Rushmore House, in that village, is the charming prep school Sandroyd, which has reached a position of some eminence in recent years. King John gave Tollard the epithet Royal during his many hunting trips across Cranborne Chase. He used to meet at a wych elm in what are now Larmer Gardens to the south of the village. Larmer Gardens were created by the Pitt-Rivers family, and are open to the public. General Pitt-Rivers was a well-known archaeologist who discovered and restored King John's house in the village. After Rotherley Down is Winkelbury, with its 40 ft ramparts, providing views across both Hampshire and Dorset. Beyond it is Berwick St John, which brings the Oxdrove bridleway to an end.

OS Map: 184

Accommodation with stables:
Grovelly Riding Centre, Ditchampton, Wilton. Mrs F. Ross, Wishford House, near Salisbury, Wiltshire SP2 0PQ. Tel: 0722 790486. Mrs D. Bradshaw, Home Farm, High Street, Hinton, Salisbury, Wiltshire SP3 6DR. Tel: Hinton 519. Mrs M. Holmes, Formakin Farm, Gotham, Cranborne, Dorset BH21 5QW. Tel: Verwood 822713.

Vets:
Avon Lodge Veterinary Group, Avon Lodge, 21 Stratford Road, Salisbury, Wiltshire SP1 3JN. Tel: 0722 412211.

Farriers:
B. H. Alford RSS AFCL FWCF, 31 Waterditchampton, Wilton, Salisbury, Wiltshire SP2 0JA. Tel: Salisbury 742538.

Further Help:
Mrs Elizabeth Hinings, British Horse Society, Home Farm, Sutton Veny, Warminster, Wiltshire BA12 7AX. Tel: 0985 40021. John Rogers, Bridleways Officer, Wiltshire County Council, County Hall, Bythesea Road, Trowbridge, Wiltshire BA14 8JG. Tel: 0225 753641 x 3345.

The Ridgeway

The Countryside Commission's Ridgeway is based on, but different from, the old Ridgeway. The old Ridgeway, connecting the west of England with the North Sea, followed the scarp of the Vale of the White Horse before making the steep descent to the Goring Gap. It was too high a road for the Romans, who needed constant watering, and they only used it in parts. At Goring it turned into the lower, but even more ancient Icknield Way. The great forts of the western section, Barbury, Liddington, Uffington and Segsbury were built to hold the Ridgeway as a trading route for the Beaker People and protect them from attacks from the north. Judging by their remains these merchant immigrants from the Iberian Peninsular and the west coast of continental Europe must have been a highly cultured and beautiful people.

The bridleway, opened in 1973, is along the Countryside Commission's Ridgeway. It runs for 50 miles from near Avebury in Wiltshire to Streatley on the River Thames in Oxfordshire, and takes three days to ride, based on a rule of eight hours feeding, eight hours rest and eight in the saddle. It is almost entirely contained within the North Wessex Area of Outstanding Natural Beauty, downs which consist of over 1,000 square miles of smooth grassy chalk hills. The route is not always clearly marked, but is soon to be designated one of the new National Trails, which will help. It is rideable by all types of horse and pony, and the springy turf along the gallops is hailed as the best in the world by enthusiastic racing buffs. However, use by tractors and lunatics in four-wheel drive vehicles tear it up and scar it with ruts, and wet chalk can be extremely slippery.

The start is at Overton Hill on the A4. The nearby Avebury Circle, which surrounds the village of Avebury, is the most important archaeological site of its type in the country. This Bronze Age megalith was built by the Beaker people in about 1800 BC, some 200 years before the major stones were added to Stonehenge. Sarsen stones

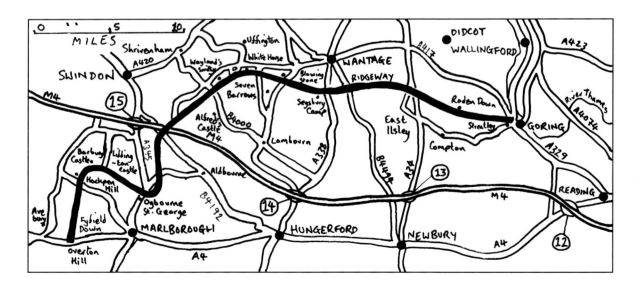

were used, weighing up to 40 tons, to make a circle with a diameter of just over three quarters of a mile, with an avenue of more stones leading towards Overton Hill. The stones seem to have been chosen for their pleasing shapes, perhaps representing male and female figures. Avebury itself consists of St James's Church which has Saxon origins, an Elizabethan manor house, and some delightful cottages with gardens in front. The Manor, with its beautiful panelling and the fine topiary in its gardens, is open to the public. There is also a museum in the village. Much of the building material used here comes from the circle, which has constantly been desecrated over the years. One of the stones, which was lying on its side, was moved in 1938, and the man who originally toppled it in the early fourteenth century was found underneath, with money from the reign of Edward I in his belt, and a pair of the earliest known British scissors. From this we deduce that when not trying to pinch magic stones he was a barber.

The Ridgeway from here is dotted with Sarsen stones. Sarsen is a corruption of the word saracen, meaning foreign. These odd weatherbeaten pieces of sandstone are all that remain of the siliceous rock which must have covered the chalk at one time. Some local people call them grey wethers, because they look like sheep. As well as Avebury parts of Stonehenge are Sarsen. However, the larger rocks at Stonehenge, not on the Ridgeway but always worth visiting, are made of a peculiar blue granite star stone from the Prescelly Mountains in Pembrokeshire. Sarsen is often apparent as building stone used in older cottages along the Ridgeway. Fyfield Down is a 600 acre National Nature Reserve nearby noted for its Sarsen stones, where the Avebury stones probably came from.

The Sanctuary on Overton Hill where the Ridgeway begins, at the end of the stone avenue, opposite a transport café, is a smaller version of Avebury. The track goes to the east of Silbury Hill, a 130 ft high man made mound, the largest in western Europe. It was built about 1600 BC, the same time as Stonehenge was being completed. Nobody knows why it was constructed, and the zealous archaeologists, including a team from the BBC, who have tunnelled into it in search of longships have always returned empty- if not a little grubby-handed.

About an hour into the ride you reach Barbury Castle, which looms at the top of magical Hackpen Hill. It is a large Iron Age fort of about 11 acres, which went on to be used by the Saxons and the Romans as well. The name Barbury comes from the Anglo-Saxon Beranbyrg, meaning Bera's Hill. The Battle of Beranburgh was fought just to the north of the Castle in 566 AD. The Saxons, who were invading Britain at that time, defeated the British, pushing them back into the Kingdom of Wessex. At 880 ft, the Castle has views across the valley of the river Ray to the Vale of the White Horse, which is the valley of the river Ock. The Sarsen stone with the plaques commemorates the writers Richard Jefferies who often walked around this area, and a nineteenth-century railwayman and poet called Alfred Williams. One of Wiltshire's white horses was carved in 1838 on Hackpen Hill. You will be unable to see it in its full glory because it is directly below you. Several white horses like this were carved during the nineteenth century, and this is one of the few which have survived.

Follow Smeathes Ridge to Ogbourne St George and the A345. Ogbourne St Andrew and Ogbourne Maizey are close, and some of the cottages in the three Ogbournes date from before 1600. The Manor House in Ogbourne Maizey is especially fine, and the Norman Church in Ogbourne St Andrew is unusual for having a prehistoric barrow in its churchyard. The Ridgeway continues by Aldbourne Chase and its attractive woods, and come towards Snap. Snap village was cleared of people during the nineteenth century to make more pasture land for the sheep. Ironically, the origin of the name Snap is a Viking word indicating poor grazing for sheep. The track goes on over Liddington Hill to Liddington Castle, which is a 40-ft high Iron Age rampart and ditch. The spot has good views over three counties. Like Barbury Castle a plaque commemorates the writer Richard Jefferies here, and once again the poet Alfred Williams. If you are inspired to visit Jefferies' home it is in Coate, a few miles away. The village of Liddington nearby has a thirteenth-century church, a

seventeenth-century manor house, and some pretty thatched cottages. After crossing the B4192 and the M4 you go through some woods to the Shepherds Rest in Foxhill, the only pub on the Ridgeway. The stretch of track from Foxhill, past strip lynchets, to Bishopstone, is deeply rutted by tractors.

You pass quite near Ashdown House, which was built for the 1st Lord Craven towards the end of the seventeenth century. Now owned by the National Trust, its four storeys are split chalk blocks with stone quoins: 'The perfect doll's house,' as Pevsner put it. It has a mansard roof and cupola with a golden ball. The deer park in front of the house was the property of the Abbots of Glastonbury in the Middle Ages. The large oval enclosure once went round the upper wood to the south of the house. You could also take a detour to Alfred's

Sarsen stones in Avebury, dragged from Fyfield Down by the Beakerpeople in about 1800 BC

Castle on Swinley Down, which is a pre-historic enclosure. The earthen rampart and ditch surround some 2½ acres, and the old entrance was in the south east corner. Sarsen boulders were used to face the bank, but many of these were broken up (by lighting bonfires underneath) to build Ashdown House. The Castle was a defended farm-stead, rather than a hill fort, and traces of pots from periods ranging from the Iron Age, through the Saxons, to the time of the Romans have been found within it. After it you go past Ashbury and cross the B4000.

Unless you have a little Celtic magic in your veins Wayland Smithy probably won't reshoe your beast. It is in a spinney to the left of the track and consists of two neolithic long barrows built within 50 years of each other containing no less than 22 bodies, as the 1962 excavations discovered. There is a legend of a smithy, though. Sir Walter Scott mentions it in *Kenilworth*. 'You must tie your horse to that upright stone that has a ring in it and then you must whistle three times and lay your money on that flat stone and then sit down amongst the bushes and not look for ten minutes. Then you will hear the hammer clink. Then say your prayers and you will find your money gone and your horse shod.' Wayland the Smith is a Scandinavian mythological figure who made invincible weapons. Unfortunately horses do not fit through the gate provided, so presumably Wayland is out of business. Just beyond it is Uffington Castle, which was an Iron Age fort occupied between 500 and 300 BC. The oval-shaped eight acre site is now managed and owned by the National Trust, which is engaged in its restoration. On a clear day it has views over five counties.

To see the well-known White Horse of Uffington on Whitehorse Hill from the best

The Ridgeway crossing Hackpen Hill.

perspective, you must leave the Ridgeway and follow the B4507. Although the White Horse might be an Iron Age work, or to commemorate the goddess Epona, protectoress of horses, and has been compared to representations of horses on Iron Age coins, the local legend is that it was carved by King Alfred's troops after he successfully beat the Danes in 871 at a battle on the Downs. It looks as if it is struggling to climb out of the combe beneath the hill called The Manger. Due to the natural drift and the riotous party which goes with its annual cleaning by local villagers, its shape has altered over the centuries.

Just to your right there are the famous Lambourn Gallops. This is a long stretch of carefully manicured turf on Kingston Warren Down and Wellbottom Down, designed to be springy and firm for use by the racehorses which are stabled in Lambourn. The ground is privately owned, but there is a strictly signed ride across it through markers of black and white posts. To your left, beyond the White Horse, is the flat-topped Dragon Hill, which experts say is a natural formation, where St George slew the dragon. Also close is Rams Hill. This used to be the site of a prehistoric fort with pallisaded ramparts. It is now invisible from the ground, but can be seen from the air.

The Blowing Stone is at the bottom of Blowingstone Hill which you cross. It is a Sarsen boulder with a natural hole in it about 18 ins long. If you blow it in a special way it makes a loud note, which will not only scare the horses, but can be heard from a couple of miles away on a still day. King Alfred is

The ancient Ridgeway, here on the southern extension at West Lavington, has long been a Romany route. (John Watts.)

supposed to have called his men to battle with it. Thomas Hughes who lived in the area mentioned it in his book *Tom Brown's Schooldays*, though he said it was in a garden of an inn. The Seven Barrows, the Long Barrow and Idelbush Barrow are all Bronze Age burial sites in the area. Their rather clipped shape comes from the fact that they are mown in September to improve the local flora. The Seven Barrows contain at least 35 burial grounds. The word 'idel' in Idelbush is the Anglo-Saxon for 'empty' thus warning off the graverobbers.

The Ridgeway goes round Childrey Warren, and a giant dip called the Devil's Punchbowl. Just after Hill Barn to the right is the mast in Sparsholt Firs which is part of Britain's telephone network. It was set up by the RAF during the Second World War. The track to the Letcombes takes you across the B4001, along gallops, and past Gramps Hill and Parsonage Hill. Although Letcombe Bassett is smaller than Letcombe Regis it has made its mark more firmly on history. Before going to Ireland, Jonathan Swift spent his last summer in England there at the Rectory, writing *Verses on Myself* and being visited by Alexander Pope. One of the local industries was growing watercress in Letcombe Brook, and 'Bassett Cress!' was a London street-cry a hundred years after Swift's time. Thomas Hardy then used the village, while staying in it, as Cresscombe, in his last novel *Jude the Oscure*.

After the Courthill Ridgeway Centre, roughly two thirds of the entire trip, and so reached at the end of the second day, is another prehistoric settlement, Segsbury Fort, also called Letcombe Castle. From it can be seen the cooling towers of Didcot Power Station, which will be perhaps as inexplicable and rich with archaeological potential one day as Segsbury Fort is now.

You have to follow the A338 briefly to come to Whitehouse Farm. The next road to cross is the B4494. Grims Ditch, to the left, actually runs all the way from Lattin Down to Streatley, roughly parallel with the Ridgeway. It was a defensive boundary to stop the raiders who lived in the Vale of the White Horse rustling the cattle and sheep of the gentle folk who lived at the eastern end of the Berkshire Downs. Grim was another name for the great god Woden.

The Monument on Betterton Down commemorates Lord Wantage VC KCB (1832–1901) who was a great landowner in the area, and took enormous interest in the welfare of his 28,000 acre estate and its people. The spinneys and hedgerows you can see from the Ridgway were mostly planted at his instigation. He was also responsible for building a model village complete with farm, a statue of King Alfred in the market place at Wantage, and a gallery in the town's Old Corn Exchange with pictures of all holders of the Victoria Cross, including himself. 664 ft Scutchamer Knob used to be a barrow, the burial place of a local chieftain called Cwichelm, but it was dug up in 1842 and destroyed. The word 'scutch' means to beat out, and is usually used in connection with retted flax. The track continues near East and West Hendred, which grew to be important local economic centres because the stream which ran between them, Ginge Brook, was powerful enough to turn water mills.

Over the brow of Gore Hill there is a tunnel underneath the A34. This is followed by more gallops, and after the Fair Mile you descend into the Thames Valley. Streatley, which is at the bottom of Roden Down, is generally held to be prettier than Goring, just across the river. It has some attractive Georgian cottages, and a nineteenth-century gabled malt house. It lies in the Goring Gap, between the Chilterns and the North Wessex Downs, and the chalk bluff Streatley Hill rises directly behind the town. If you cross the bridge to Goring you can continue your ride along the Swan's Way.

There is an unofficial but well known westwards extension called The Great Ridgeway, which goes down through south-west Wiltshire from Avebury, towards Devizes, West Lavington and ending near Tisbury. An official extension planned to go to Dorset will almost certainly use this route. Furthermore, Oxfordshire and Wiltshire County Councils publish leaflets with maps of 'circular walks' off the Ridgeway. Almost all of these can be ridden. They are about five to ten miles long, but linked with riding sections of the Ridgeway itself, and could constitute alternative long-distance rides.

OS Maps: 173, 174, 165, 175.

Horse-box Parking:
Barbury Castle Country Park, just south of Swindon. Fox Hill, near the M4 south east of Swindon. Sparsholt Firs, on the B4001. Bury Down, a minor road west of the A34.

Accommodation with stables:
Mrs A. Yarrow, Gwenfa Fields, Red Lion Hill, The Lee, Great Missenden, Buckinghamshire, HP16 9NF. Mrs S. Burgess, 2 Lily Cottages, Hillesden, near Buckingham, Buckinghamshire MK18 4DD. Tel: 0280 816991. Mrs Skinner, Silverdown Riding Holidays, Harwell, Oxfordshire OX11 0LU. Tel: 0235 835377. Mrs C. Brake, Oak Farm, Maidensgrove, Henley-on-Thames, Oxfordshire RG9 6EX. Tel: Nettlebed 641368. Mrs A. Park, The Coach House, Letcombe Regis, Wantage, Oxfordshire. Tel: 0235 766561. Mrs V. Haigh, Home Farm, Charlton, Wantage, Oxfordshire OX12 7HE. Tel: 0235 833300. Miss Sarah West, Ford Farm Stables, Aldbourne, Marlborough, Wiltshire. Tel: Marlborough 40110. Mrs S. Hanmer, Wick Down Cottage, Broad Hinton, Swindon, Wiltshire. Tel: 0672 54740. Mrs Freeston, Smiths Farm, Bushton, Swindon, Wiltshire SN4 9PX. Tel: 0793 73285. Foxlynch Junior Training Centre, Foxlynch, Ogbourne St George, Marlborough, Wiltshire SN8 1TD. Tel: 0672 84307. Mrs Wadsworth, The Craven, Fernham Road, Uffington, Farringdon, Oxfordshire SN7 7RD. Tel: 0367 82449. Mrs Godfrey (Caravan), White Horse Stables, Goosey Glebe Smallholding, Goosey, Wantage, Oxfordshire. Tel: 0367 78806 or 0235 87492.

Vets:
Belmont House Veterinary Service, 70 Wilcot Road, Pewsey, Wiltshire SN9 5EL Tel: 0672 63413. C. J. Frank, Sunwillow Farm, Childrey, Wantage, Oxfordshire. Tel: 0235 59242.

Farriers:
Mr Jeremy Baker, c/o Farrier Unit 14, The Wagon Yard, London Road, Marlborough, Wiltshire. Tel: Marlborough 53961. Alfred Hall, 2 Spanswick Cottage, Holbourn Hill, Hetesmbe Bassett, Wantage, Oxfordshire OX12 9LR. Tel: Wantage 65419.

Further Help:
Mrs Penelope Reid, British Horse Society Bridleways Officer, Morewood House, Hampstead Marshall, Newbury, Berkshire RG15 0JD. Tel: 0488 58823. Mrs Joan Allen, Secretary, Long Distance Riding Group (Ridgeway), Buckland Grange, St Leonards, Tring, Hertfordshire HP23 6NP. Tel: 0240 29222.

The South

The South Downs Way near Harting Hill.
(R. J. Wilson.)

The Swan's Way

The Swan's Way runs for 65 miles, mostly through Buckinghamshire, from Goring-on-Thames in Oxfordshire to the Salcey Forest on the border with Northamptonshire. Going along the spring line on the chalk scarp of the Chilterns from Goring to Princes Risborough, it follows the Ridgeway extension, or the old Icknield Way. Despite the packaging and neat logos of the Countryside Commission and local authorities, all these bridleways have roots in an Anglo-Saxon past, if not earlier. The Icknield Way joined the old Ridgeway to link the south-west of England with the North Sea. The latter part of the Swan's Way, from Princes Risborough up towards Northampton, winds its way through the Vale of Aylesbury.

The Way, which was opened in September 1987 and takes four days to ride, crosses a wide variety of scenery, from the river Thames at Goring, through woods of beech, cherry lime and hornbeam, along the Chilterns, past Aylesbury and on into the Ouse valley. Buckinghamshire County Council publish a descriptive leaflet with a route map and information about stabling and accommodation. The ride is well-signed, waymarked with the Swan's Way logo, and easy to follow. All the main roads can be crossed straight with good vision, which is one area where bridleways planned by county engineers score over unofficial rides. It is generally negotiable all the year round by horse or pony, and its surface includes chalk, clay, gravel and tarmac.

Goring started as the ford where the Ridgeway met the Icknield Way, but became extremely fashionable during the Edwardian era as a Thameside spot. The houses along the river stand testament to the importance of a mansion in that area in those days. Cleeve Road in the town itself is the start of the ride, and you head north along the bank of the river Thames, beside the main Oxford–Reading railway line. The first place you go through is South Stoke. One of Brunel's finest railway bridges lies just north of South Stoke, and if you approach it quietly you may see a student engineer taking notes beside it. The Way then goes near North Stoke along part of the B4009. There is a track from Kaffirs leading to the crossing of the A4074, which is the most difficult road on the whole ride, with especially poor visibility. However, the track is easy to miss, and if you do carry on up to the main road, go left along the verge, and then go right up the minor road. You go through the delightfully named Drunken Bottom leaving Coblers Hill to your left.

After crossing the Ridgeway you come to Grims Ditch, which once marked the boundary between two Iron Age kingdoms. Ditches like these, often called 'Devil's Ditch' are also found in Hertfordshire, Buckinghamshire and elsewhere in Oxfordshire. After Blenheim Farm is the A423 and then Potters Farm. You may have noticed by now the aeroplanes, which come from the nearby base at RAF Benson. The Queen's Flight is stationed there, so don't forget to wave. Nearby is the pretty village of Ewelme. St Mary's Church, the school and the almshouses were all built in the fifteenth century by the Earl of Suffolk, largely at the instigation of his wife, Alice, who was the granddaughter of the poet Chaucer. After Down Farm is the Britwell Salome to Stonor road. Stonor Park itself is quite close. The great catholic family Stonor have lived there since Anglo-Saxon times.

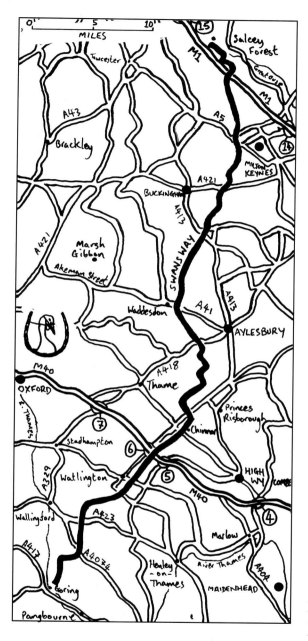

and the public can troop round and view it only one day per week.

The Swan's Way crosses the B480 and goes past Icknield House. It passes to the west of Watlington Hill, which rises to a height of 686 ft and is famous for its yew trees. Cut into the side of the hill is the White Mark, a vast isosceles triangle, managed by the National Trust. In 1794 a local gentleman named Mr Horne who had always been disappointed that Watlington Church didn't have a spire decided to do something about it. He carved the symbol directly in line with the church and his window, so that from his house it looks as if there is a spire. Watlington grew to some importance in the area because it was on the Icknield Way. It would be a good place to stop for the first night. The Victorian and Georgian cottages here, in pretty chequered red brick and flint give a charming feel to this little town. It also has a good seventeenth-century market hall.

Putting Shirburn Wood to your east you go near Lewknor, which is worth seeing for its church. However, perhaps it would be better to leave the noise of the M40 as far behind as possible. After going through the motorway underpass, and crossing the A40 which is dominated by the 784 ft Beacon Hill, you come to Aston Rowant. The Aston Rowant National Nature Reserve is popular among botanists, especially for its yew scrub, privet and juniper. Kingston Wood is on the other side of the Way from Kingston Blount, which is next to the hamlet of Cromwell. The next biggish town is Chinnor, which the track skirts. Despite being put off by Chinnor's ghastly cement works you should see it for one of the most important Decorated churches in the country, with exceptional stained glass windows and brasses.

Bledlow Great Wood, through which the

The Georgian facade of the present house hides a thirteenth-century core, and some unique domestic architecture dating from the Middle Ages. The view is also magnificent. Lord and Lady Camoys live there, county boundary runs, is along the Way on the right. Bledlow Cop is 799 ft above sea-level, and has a round barrow on top. Bledlow itself, on the western scarp of the Chilterns, is steeped in history. Holy Trinity Church, with its distinctive flint-faced walls, is Norman in origin. The River Lyde rises in the church yard, and flows through beds of watercress in a village of herringbone brick houses. The Bledlow Cross in Wainhill was probably carved at the instigation of a local landowner in imitation of the more famous nearby seventeenth-century White-leaf Cross.

Under one railway line and across another, through Pitch Green, over the B4009 and in and out of Ford, all in an effort to go round Princes Risborough, a good old-fashioned market town. This is where the Icknield Way leaves the Swan's Way to go towards Wendover. Fifteenth-century Chequers, the prime minister's country house is nearby, but it is not open to the public. It was left in trust to the nation by Lord Fareham in 1917, for use by future prime ministers. Lloyd George was its first tenant. If you want to see it there's a pleasant footpath crossing the field in front of it. The Swan's Way goes on to Ilmer, where you negotiate a third railway line, and which contains St Peter's Church, one of the oldest within the Oxford diocese, with parts of the original Norman building. It was rebuilt in 1350, and the spire was restored in 1979. After the A4129 is Owlswick, Kimble Wick, and a short diversion to Bishopstone if you are interested. By now you may well be reaching the end of your second day.

You reach the A418 in Stone, which is notable for the Norman font in its church, with its representations of human heads, birds, animals and fish. From Stone to Waddesdon all the land belongs to the Wad-

desdon Estate. This includes Hartwell, Eythrope Park beside the River Thame and Upper Winchenden. Although the Swan's Way doesn't go through this village it has a twelfth-century church with lovely views of the Chilterns and the Thame valley. If you have the time, you must see that, and Nether Winchenden House and gardens.

The Way crosses the A41, which goes to Waddesdon. The church in this village, which was originally Norman, has an imposing nave in three arches. Look out for the giant statue of the knight, believed to be the tomb of Sir Roger Dynham. The recess above the door in the porch holds a delightful statue of St Michael.

The most fabulous place in the area is standing on a 600 ft hill. Waddesdon Manor, which is run by the National Trust, was built in the style of a renaissance French Chateau for Baron Ferdinand de Rothschild during the 1870s. The house contains a superb collection of seventeenth and eighteenth-century French artefacts, as well as paintings by Ruben, Reynolds and Gainsborough. The ceiling by de Witt is particularly stunning. The gardens, which include both Sika deer and an extraordinary rococo aviary, have some outstanding views.

The Swan's Way goes near Quainton which has a number of places of interest, especially its 100 ft high, early nineteenth-century windmill. Above Quainton, on 613 ft Quainton Hill, there are the remains of a medieval settlement. This spot is meant to be the haunt of goblins and fairies, not to mention the odd headless horseman. There is a Roman road, now known as Gypsy Lane, with a stone commemorating the death in 1641 of a king of the Gypsies.

According to legend, North Marston's spring has the gift to heal. Because of it the village used to be a centre of pilgrimage for the sick and injured. The village church was restored during the nineteenth century. This is nothing extraordinary for the Victorians restored hundreds of churches, often in a ham-fisted manner, but this restoration was paid for by Queen Victoria. A local miser had died leaving her his fortune, and, faced with something of a dilemma of protocol, she immediately put it to the community's use.

The Swan's Way continues over Christmas Gorse, across the A413 to Swanbourne, which features a number of black and white cottages. It was built almost entirely from the seventeenth century onwards after Cromwell's troops destroyed the old village during the Civil War. In it you go over the B4032. Further on you come to Whaddon Chase, over which the A421 runs. It used to be covered in forest and was a great royal hunting ground. Three ancient woods still survive, Thickbare, Broadway and Thrift. Unfortunately you will only go through the latter. Directly after it is Whaddon. The village itself is on quite a high plateau, and was once used as a camp by the Romans. This was where Edmund Spenser wrote some of his classic work *The Faerie Queen*.

More suitable for swans than horses, the bleak fringes of Otmoor.

Snelshall Priory, which was a Benedictine Abbey founded in 1166, and which lasted until the dissolution of the monasteries, is marked by earthworks on the path just to the east of Whaddon.

The Way passes along the edge of Oakhill Wood and past Shenley Wood before coming to Shenley Church End. Loughton, beyond it, is the beginning of Milton Keynes's series of green belts, preserved in an effort to make the town look green and pleasant. The ponds you pass, Bancroft Lake and Lodge Lake, are two of the four balancing lakes which stop Loughton Brook from flooding.

Milton Keynes, on the grand Union Canal, is looking forward to a population of 200,000 by the end of the century. It was begun in 1967 to relieve London's housing difficulties and to be a base for commerce in Hertfordshire. Communication links to the town are excellent, as you are bound to notice when you negotiate both the A5 and the main London–Scotland railway.

Bradwell Abbey nearby was founded at about the same time as Snelshall Priory, and by the same people. Its priory became a farm after the dissolution, and the only original part now is the chapel, which dates from the fourteenth century. The farmhouse, which was build in the seventeenth century, has become a City Discovery Centre, with 'environmental interpretation facilities'. The windmill in Bradwell, now a working museum, was built in 1817 and in its professional capacity lasted for 60 years. You cross the A422 before Bradville, and after New Bradwell the Swan's Way goes along a railway which was closed in 1964. It leaves it again at Stantonbury, and briefly follows the course of the Great Ouse. Linford Wood, the M1 at Tathall End, and Stokepart Wood near Stoke to it close.

The Three Shires Way

In October 1990 a new section of bridleway was opened. Linking with the Swan's Way at Tathall End, in the Salcey Forest, it extends 35 miles through Buckinghamshire, Bedfordshire, Northamptonshire, the old county of Huntingdonshire and Cambridgeshire, to end at Grafham Water. The route is open to walkers and cyclists (though not motor cyclists). Much of it is on clay, so it will be muddy at times, but it is clearly signposted and runs along a number of ancient tracks through some very old woodland and pretty villages, the first of which is Emberton with its attractive country park.

The ride crosses the Great Ouse, into Northamptonshire, at Laverton Mill and follows the river into Bedfordshire at Three Shires Wood. Here it joins Forty Foot Lane, an ancient routeway of pre-Roman origins, which is now a beautiful green lane. Half way along Forty Foot Lane is Podington Airfield which is now used for high-speed drag-racing. This is a very noisy sport and it is worth telephoning 071-486 7676 to check on race times.

The way visits one of Bedfordshire's major earthworks, Yielden Castle, then crosses into Cambridgeshire near Covington before following minor roads, green lanes and drove roads, traversing the escarpment and dropping down to Grafham Water. It joins up with a circular ride round the reservoir, a site of special scientific interest and a resting place for migrating waterfowl. The village of Grafham itself is the convenient place to end the ride.

OS Maps: 175, 165, 152 and 153

Horse-box parking:
Goring car park on the corner of the High Street and Cleeve Road. Where the Britwell Salome to Stonor road intersects the Swan's Way, near Watlington. The A41 Waddesdon layby, and riders must use the northern verge of the A41 to join the Swan's Way, and recross at the crossroads if going south. Christmas Gorse, just off the A413. By the pub on the road between New Bradwell and Newport Pagnell. In Salcey Forest itself. There are two turnings off the B526 to the Salcey Forest, one in Northamptonshire and one in Buckinghamshire: take the Buckinghamshire turning.

Accommodation with stables:
Mr and Mrs C. E. Lane, The Manor House, Weston Road, Lewknor, near Watlington, Oxfordshire OX9 5RU. Tel: 0844 51680. Mrs D. Belcher (Grazing only), Hale Farm, Benson, Wallingford, Oxfordshire OX9 6NE. Tel: 0491 36818. Mrs T. Shadbolt, Crowell End, Spriggs Alley, near Chinnor, Oxfordshire OX9 4BT. Tel: 0844 52726. Mrs Grizelda Block, Bridleways Farm, Meadle, Aylesbury, Buckinghamshire HP17 9UG. Tel: 0844 46368. Mrs E. Jeffrey, The Gables, Skittle Green, Bledlow, Aylesbury, Buckinghamshire HP17 9PJ. Tel: 0844 44392. Mrs C. Ramsay, The Bell House Barn, Crowbrook Road, Askett, Princes Risborough, Aylesbury, Buckinghamshire HP17 9LS. Tel: 0844 46107. Mr T. F. Robinson, Marstonfields Farm, North Marston, Buckingham, Buckinghamshire MK18 3PG. Tel: 0296 67215. Mrs P. Crawford, Laurel Farm, Singleborough, Milton Keynes, Buckinghamshire MK17 0RF. Tel: 0296 712282. Mrs S. Phillips, Holywell Farm, Thornton Road, Nash, Buckinghamshire MK17 0EY. Tel: 0908 501769. Mr R. H. G. Corner (term time only), Grange Farm, Beachampton, Milton Keynes, Buckinghamshire MK19 6DZ. Tel: 0908 563275. Mr and Mrs N. Stacey, Home Farm, Hanslope Road, Castlethorpe, Milton Keynes, Buckinghamshire MK19 7HD. Tel: 0908 510208/510985. Mr and Mrs K. Adams, Chantry Farm, Hanslope, Milton Keynes, Buckinghamshire MK19 7HL. Tel: 0908 510269.

Vets:
R. E. Baskerville, East Lodge, Aston Rowant, Oxfordshire OX9 5SN. Tel: Kingston Blount 52090. C. E. Hargreaves, Dartmouth House, Olney, Buckinghamshire. Tel: 0234 711473.

Farriers:
W. Smith RSS AFCL FWCF, 23 Watcombe Road, Watlington, Oxfordshire OX9 5QJ. Tel: Watlington 2872. T. Fraser Mackenzie Head, Hawkswood, Great Brickhill, Milton Keynes, Buckinghamshire MK17 8AL. Tel: Great Brickhill 417.

Further Help:
Anne Leigh, Executive Officer, Bridleways Committee, British Horse Society, British Equestrian Centre, Kenilworth, Warwickshire CV8 2LR. Tel: 0203 696697. Mrs Brenda Wickham, British Horse Society County Bridleways Officer, Chiltern Cottage, Upway, Chalfont, St Peter's, Buckinghamshire SL9 0AS. Tel: 0753 882827. Ms C. M. Day, Rural Management Division, Department of Property, Cambridgeshire County Council, Shire Hall, Castle Hill, Cambridge CB3 0AP. Tel: 0223 317445.

The South Downs Way

This 80 mile path in the gently undulating countryside of the South Downs was opened in July 1972. It was Britain's first official long-distance bridleway, and by and large it is not a difficult ride, though it may take three or four days to complete. It was designed with both riders and walkers in mind, and there are rights of way for its entire length from Eastbourne to the borders of Hampshire. The ride is well established, but one needs to be able to read a map, and watch out for signposts, especially the low concrete plinths which mark the Way in East Sussex. The oak post signs of West Sussex are much easier to follow. Riders are also warned that road crossings can be dangerous. The South Downs Way traverses some of Britain's busiest trunk roads, notably the A23, A24, A27 and A29.

This is a bridleway for all seasons, though even in summer there can be a biting wind on the top. After heavy rain it can become extremely muddy, and in certain places there has been erosion from over-use of the path by riders and walkers in these conditions. In general the going is easy, being mainly chalky with occasional clay and flints. Little remains of the original grass track, and with the tarmac of the roads there are areas which can be hard on soft soles. In these cases it would be worth bringing a leather pad for the soles of your horse's hooves. There are also motorbike traps. These are of a design approved by the British Horse Society, but considered hazardous by many Pony Club district commissioners, and an illegal obstruction by highway authorities in some other counties. It is the problem with all bridleways: horses and motorbicycles don't mix.

The South Downs Way is the most popular long-distance ride in Britain. The scenery is

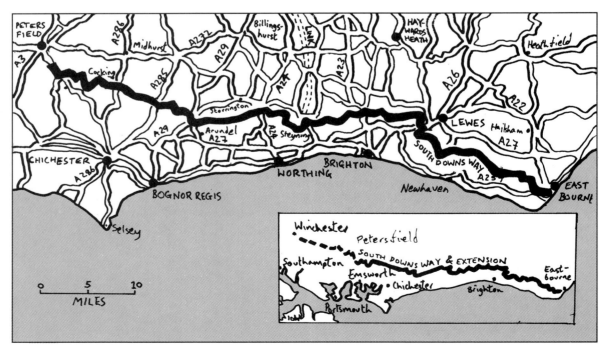

superb. In the words of Chris White, the regional bridleways officer, 'like riding on the roof of the world'. As you forsake the flint and chalk strewn paths to cross the famous fishing rivers Ouse and Arun, with their lilies and reeds, you are often assailed by teal, wigeon and snipe. At the start, in Eastbourne, riders have the edge over walkers because although the footpath which winds steeply upwards to Beachy Head looks dramatic, the view from the bridleway is perhaps the more spectacular. Having crossed the East Dean road the Way climbs steeply up 659 ft Willingdon Hill before reaching Jevington. It is particularly important, if you want to avoid missing your way in the first few miles, to follow the concrete plinths, which mark the route most carefully.

After Jevington, and as you go over Wilmington Hill, keep an eye out for the Long Man of Wilmington which the walkers will miss. He is 231 ft tall, and may date from as long ago as the sixth century, or he is possibly a representation of King Harold of the Saxons. The great figure, which holds two staves in his hands, was first recorded in 1779. From Windover Hill can be seen one of the finest views of the South Downs Way.

The next part of the ride is the descent into Alfriston and the crossing of Cuckmere River. Just before Alfriston the bridleway is joined by the footpath. The fourteenth-century church which dominates the town, standing on an Anglo-Saxon mound, is known locally as the Cathedral of the Downs. Much in Alfriston is ancient. The Star Inn is one of the oldest in England, dating from the thirteenth century, and do look out for the weathered medieval market cross. The town also has the first ever National Trust building, a fourteenth-centry clergy house.

Leaving Alfriston there is a climb to Firle Beacon. At 713 ft this is one of the highest points on the ride, and has fine views in all directions. It is as a honeypot to bees for trippers on sunny weekends, and also attracts the hang-gliding fraternity. Nearby is the home of the Gage family, Firle Place, built from Caen stone with a Horsham stone roof in the eighteenth century. At the bottom of the meandering downhill path is the first real hazard of the ride. Having negotiated the A26, Newhaven Road, you will find a railway crossing at Southease. Although it is provided with a telephone to call the signal box up the line, many people find its self-service barrier rather frightening, especially if several horses are crossing at the same time. Directly after the hamlet of Southease through which runs the river Ouse, is Rodwell, with its popular pub the Abergavenny Arms. For those not lured from the path, there is the ascent of Iford Hill, up Mill lane. This is a possible place to end your first day, so you might consider resting the horses about now.

Shortly after the hill a local track branches off to Kingston. You could go on here to the interesting town of Lewes. If you don't follow this detour, after Iford Hill is Newmarket Hill, and then the descent to the A27, during which you go beneath a railway line. The crossing on this road by the Newmarket Inn turn is especially bad, so take extreme care. The A27 is the main South Coast road. After it the path turns sharply over windswept Plumpton Plain. Nearby Plumpton Place is a grand sixteenth-century moated manor house, which was restored by Sir Edwin Lutyens during the 1920s. Between it and the South Downs there is a piece of woodland shaped live a V which was planted to commemorate Queen Victoria's Golden Jubilee in 1887. Plumpton race-course is quite close as well. Ditchling Beacon is the next landmark. At 813 ft it ranks high amongst the best views of the entire Way. Two and a half miles to the north is the village of Ditchling which contains a house given by Henry VIII to Anne of Cleeves. Shortly after the Beacon, past the dew ponds, you reach Keymer Post which is the border between East and West Sussex. You pass the two Clayton Windmills, nicknamed Jack and Jill, and then turn sharply through New Barn Farm before the descent to Pyecombe.

The A273 and the A23 converge at Pyecombe, and both are ghastly roads to have to cross. The new Pyecombe bypass could either make it worse, or better, according to how the new slip road is built. Pyecombe itself has an old forge, which used to be an important centre for the manufacture of shepherds crooks. A nearby point of interest is Danny, Hurstpierpoint, dating from 1593. It is an E-shaped house to honour Queen Elizabeth I who gave George Goring, its builder, the surrounding estate. It was later the home of the Campion family, and in 1918 the War Cabinet under Lloyd George met in the house to draw up terms for the armistice with Germany. It is worth checking beforehand to see if it is open. From Pyecombe the route goes out towards the charming village of Saddlescombe past the Brendon riding centre, and via West Hill. After Saddlescombe the path climbs up past a reservoir and crosses the Poynings to Brighton road. This is greatly favoured hang-gliding country. On the left there is a road leading to the spectacular Devils Dyke. Devils Dyke, which has a hotel boasting fine teas, is a V shaped cleft in the Downs (not this time in honour of Queen Victoria) with long views inland. The legend goes that the Devil, worried by the growth of Christian-ity in the Weald, started to dig a trench to the English Channel in order to flood it. A woman who was watching him held up her candle, and the Devil abandoned his project and fled, thinking it was the first rays of dawn.

The way leads on over Perching Hill and past Edburton Hill and the youth hostel. To the left is the chapel of Lancing College, headquarters and paradigm of the Woodward Schools. The neo-Gothic chapel is a carbuncular cathedral shape with a 90 ft high chalk and stone vaulted ceiling. It contains a curious hotch-potch of school memorabilia, including a rose window with symbols of all the Woodward schools in stained glass, and canopies from Eton College. The chapel is open to the public.

Keeping your eyes on the road, the next obstacle is the A283 and the bridge over the river Adur to St Botolphs. In the Middle Ages, before the river silted up, ships used the village of Bramber, just upstream, as a port. Because of this St Botolphs was once prominent in the area, but it has since decayed. However, it still has a pretty church with an Anglo-Saxon chancel arch and wall, and it is important to the South Downs Way because it is the junction with another bridle-way, described in the next chapter, the Downs Link Path, which comes from near Guildford. This would be another possible place to spend a night. Near St Botolphs is the magnificent Grade I medieval St Mary's House built in 1470, with its unusual panel-ling, and a unique painted room originally decorated for Elizabeth I.

From St Botolphs a pretty country lane takes you past Annington Farm and Annington Manor, and up Annington Hill. At the top you join the Sompting to Steyning road for a short stretch, and then go straight on, as it bends round to the right. This takes

Clear, oak sign-posts in West Sussex. (John Watts.)

you past Steyning Round Hill. The village of Steyning itself contains charming medieval gabled houses. The legend goes that the place was founded when the zealously penitent St Cuthman was pushing his ill mother from Devon in a wheelbarrow. The barrow eventually broke, and St Cuthman decided that that would be a good spot to stop and build a church. Steyning's present church, St Andrews, was built in the twelfth century, and its stained glass windows depict St Cuthman. It is also the burial ground of King Ethelwulf of Wessex, the father of King Alfred.

The Chanctonbury Ring, further on, is marked, confusingly, by a ring of beech trees. These trees stand in the mounds of the Iron Age earth works, and are often mistaken for the Ring itself. They were planted in 1760 by Charles Goring who lived at the nearby Elizabethan mansion of Wiston Park.

The Chanctonbury Ring is 783 ft above sea-level at the top, and the view stretches for 30 miles around on a good day. A hoard of Anglo-Saxon coins was once found in the area. There is a path leading to Cissbury Ring five miles away. The hump this Iron Age fort is on is as much of a landmark as the Chanctonbury beeches. Cissbury Ring, which is kept up by the National Trust, consists of two ramparts which were used from at least the end of the third century BC until after 55 BC. It was near an important flint mining centre, and a lot of pottery has been found in the area. There is also a Romano-British circular shrine from a later date.

After the Chanctonbury Ring is the village of Washington, and the hazardous A24. There are two ways through Washington and over the road, but try to use the special walkers' and riders' bridge by the church. It is a short dog leg to the north, and not only saves you from the vagaries of the traffic, but diverts you away from the rubbish tip you would otherwise have to pass half way up Highden Hill. The stretch between Highden Hill and Amberley Mount commands great views of the Weald and the North Downs. There are also a plethora of smaller bridleways to tempt you from the South Downs Way.

Just to the west of Storrington, below you to the north, is Parham House. It is a beautiful Elizabethan pile situated in a deer park. St Peter's church stands in its grounds. The house contains an important collection of portraits from the sixteenth to the eighteenth centuries, fine furniture, tapestries and rare needlework. The great hall is worth seeing for its ceiling and windows. There is a beautiful walled garden with herbaceous borders, herb garden and orchard, as well as seven acres of pleasure grounds with mature trees, a statuary and a lake. It was owned until earlier this century by the Bysshop family.

Coming down the steep and sometimes slippery way from Amberley Mount, you joint the B2139 into the village. Amberley has a ruined castle, which was originally built for the Bishops of Chichester in 1380, but was taken down by the roundheads during the Civil War. The shattered walls and gatehouse guard an ancient manor house. The village, which sits on a low ridge overlooks the Amberley Wild Brooks which is an area of marshland of about 30 square miles watered by the river Arun. The word 'wild' comes from 'Weald'. After passing Amberley Station, crossing the river Arun, and trotting along the road through Houghton, you will reach the dangerous A29. Having safely negotiated this you will find that the character of the South Down

Way begins to change. There is less rolling downland, studded with sheep and pierced with the cries of skylarks. From now on the emphasis will be on woody paths.

In Houghton Forest you will go near Whiteways Lodge which has loos and refreshments. Bignor Hill, directly afterwards, at 737 ft has one of the most beautiful views. It is a National Trust area and popular with trippers. Sitting on the hill is the village of Bignor with its fifteenth-century thatched and half-timbered shop. The village also has one of the largest Roman villas in Britain, dating from the second century AD. It was probably lived in for 200 years, and is important archæologically for unusually it was never sacked but simply allowed to decay. It consists of 70 buildings set in four and a half acres and features superb mosaic including one of Venus and the Gladiator, artefacts, models and underfloor heating through lead flues. If all is going according to plan Bignor or nearby is where you are staying the night.

As you come down from Bignor Hill, leaving the neolithic camp to your left, you cross the old Roman road of Stane Street, which ran from Chichester to London, or Noviomagus to Londinium as the Romans would have known them. Further inland part of it becomes the A29 which you have just crossed. Having passed Littleton Farm you go over the A285 to come up to Littleton Down. At 837 ft above sea-level, this is absolutely the highest point on the South Downs Way. Much further on, from Cocking Down at the A286, you can see the red roofs of the village of Cocking. All the cottages attached to the Cowdray Estate have their woodwork painted in a distinctive dull yellow.

After a few miles you go south under the 813 ft Linch Down, before ascending Didling Hill. Go around Treyford Hill and then

OS Maps: 197, 198, 199.

Horse-box Parking:
No box parking at the Eastbourne end – the nearest place is on the Beachy Head road on the top of the Downs. Ditchling Beacon (crowded at weekends). Jack and Jill Windmills (crowded at weekends). The junction of the South Downs Way with the A283 – parking in the old road, a sort of slip road. This also has a small picnic area with hitching posts for horses, benches, mown grass, and a water trough donated by the Annington Brickworks.

Accommodation with stables:
Mr and Mrs P. Brown, Zara Stud and Training Centre, Highleigh Road, Sidlesham, Chichester, Sussex PO20 7NR. Tel: 0243 56572/56662. Brown, Coppers Hill, Willingdon, Sussex. Tel: 0323 516518. Folkington Manor, near Polegate. Mrs Goodbody (Camping), Truleigh Hill Farm, Steyning, Sussex. Tel: 812725. M. S. Brewer, 5a Loxwood Close, Eastbourne, East Sussex BN21 0HF. Tel: Eastbourne 501805. Mrs J. Dabbs, 1 Hammonds Hill Cottages, London Road, Hassocks, West Sussex BN6 9NB. Tel: 0444 644470. Mr and Mrs J. D. Cameron, Upper Norwood Farm, Graffham, near Petworth, West Sussex GU28 0QG. Tel: 0798 6264. Mrs J. Monks, Manor Farm, Cocking, Midhurst, Sussex. Tel: 0730 812784. Mrs M. Humphrey, New House Farm, East Dean, near Chichester, Sussex. Miss B. Miles, Church Farm Cottage, Washington, Pulborough, West Sussex. Tel: Ashington 892893 (evenings). Mr and Mrs D. Jarman, Wanbarrow Farm, Bullfinch Lane, Hurstpierpoint, Sussex BN6 9ER. Tel: 0273 834110. Mrs H. Furrow, The Mill House, Rackham, Pulborough, West Sussex BH20 2EU. Tel: 0906 64159. Miss J. Lashly, Holme Farm Livery, Stansted Park, Rowland's Castle, Sussex. Tel: 0243 374238. Mrs Brightwell (Stable Flat), Oakwood, East Harting, West Sussex. Tel: Petersfield 245. Berry, Oxenbourne Farm, East Meon, Hampshire. Tel: Petersfield 239.

Vets:
John K. Hooton, The Home Farm (Quarantine Station), The Green, Wilmington, Polegate, East Sussex BN26 5SP. Tel: 0321 24562. Philcox & Pepper, 24 Chapel Hill, Lewes, Sussex BN7 2BB. Tel: 0273 472404. M. A. Ashton & Partners, Tortington Equine Centre, Arundel, West Sussex, BN18 0BG. Tel: 0903 883050. S. E. Rodgers, Moor Edge, Forest Road, Liss, Hampshire. Tel: Liss 892273.

Farriers:
J. R. Henry RSS, Steel Works, Lower Road, Eastbourne, East Sussex, BN21 1QE. Tel: Eastbourne 21938. Peter H. Fenton RSS, Club Cottage, Top Road, Arundel, West Sussex, PO18 0ED. Tel: Chichester 774524. R. P. Lockwood RSS AFCL FWCF, Forge Cottage, Church Hill, Midhurst, Sussex, GU29 9NX. Tel: Midhurst 3208.

Further Help:
Mrs V. Perrin, British Horse Society, West Sussex County Bridleways Officer, Berrylands, The Lane, Ilford, Loawood, West Sussex RH14 0PD. Tel: 0403 752591. Mrs C. White, British Horse Society, South East Regional Bridleways Officer, Primrose Lodge, Duddleswell, Uckfield, East Sussex. Tel: Nutley 2689.

down over Philliswood Down, past Buriton Farm. After Beacon Hill you come to the Harting Downs. Coming off this you cross the B2141 and the B2146. Down Forty-Acre lane and just after Sunwood farm is the Queen Elizabeth Forest. It is on the A3 just inside the Hampshire border and is the most convenient end to the ride.

The Downs Link Path

The Downs Link path, which was opened in July 1984, extends approximately 30 miles from near Guildford in Surrey, southwards, to connect the North Downs with the South Downs Way at Steyning, West Sussex. It is one of the easiest bridleways in the country and you can ride it in a weekend. The Link, and rides off it, were devised by West Sussex County Planning Department and the Surrey County Engineers Department. These are the offices usually involved in creating rides these days, though often only after a lot of pressure from interested groups or individuals. Much of the route follows an old railway line, which was bought by local authorities in 1966, and you constantly find yourself going along embankments and through cuttings. It is mostly flat but quite hard on the horses' feet. The Path changes from sandy in the north, to stony in the middle section, and fields in the south. Because of the varying geology, it has a wide range of plants, from hawthorn and carpets of bluebells on the sandy ridges to golden saxifrage and willow in the valleys. There is a plethora of bird life, including all kinds of woodpeckers, lapwings and the occasional kingfisher. The Path is waymarked and well kept up by the councils concerned. Constant maintenance is vital given the traditional likelihood of paths and rights of way to blockage, either natural or man-made, if underused or unmonitored.

The start is just to the east of St Martha's

The South Downs, near Steyning. (R. J. Wilson.)

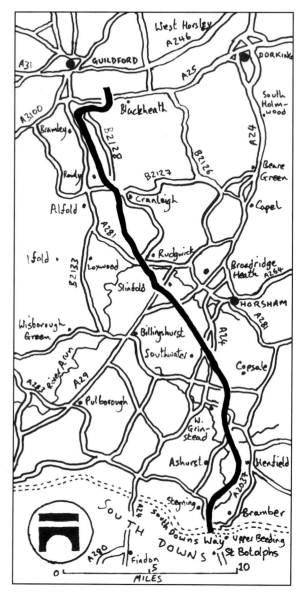

heath you cross Sample Oak Lane. Leaving Great Tangley Manor House on your right you come to Wonersh Common. At this point there is a fairly new bridleway to take you away from the frenetic B2128. The road leads to Chinthurst Hill with its superb views, and the car park, and then you reach the road by Old Chinthurst Farm. The double bridge on the right, as you go down to the railway track, was originally a single small bridge over the Wey and Arun Canal, but another bridge taking the road over the railway line was added later. Because the railway bridge just down the line was demolished, follow a short detour over the old Wey and Arun Canal Aqueduct.

The village of Bramley grew up with the coming of the canal, the railway, and then better roads. The derelict station, which you will see, is a vestige of how Bramley's fortunes turned full circle, as first the canal and then the railway left the village behind. These two dead methods of communication run beside each other past Lordshill Common to Run Common. The canal opened in 1816. It was built to connect the rivers Wey and Arun, which provided the last link in the waterway from the river Thames to the South Coast. Due to water shortages and competition from the railway it was never a huge success, and so closed in 1868. A trust was set up in 1970 to restore it to its former glory, and has been successful in places.

Run Common, grazed close by gypsies' horses, is perhaps the most open part of the route in Surrey. Then the line goes on to run close to Cranleigh Water and skirts Cranleigh, which claims to be the largest village in England. If you want to visit it turn left by the recreation centre up Village Way. In the High Street there is a crane on top of a fountain. Cranleigh was famous for its craneries, and this bird is the village's sym-

Church, which dates back to the eleventh century. Go from St Martha's Hill, southeast of Guildford, and then follow the signs towards the Tillingbourne Valley. You pass Lockner Farm Stables on the left and must take care crossing the A248. You go along the bridge over the railway line, and then onto Blackheath. At the other end of Black-

The west side of the A29 bridge. Legend has it that here the lost Roman bell tolls on stormy nights.
(Picture courtesy of Park Guest House.)

bol, as well as part of its name. Since the extinction of the crane in Britain it is also rather a sad reminder. During the Middle Ages Cranleigh was also a noted centre for hunting and falconry. It was the first village to have a hospital, and its church dates from the thirteenth century.

Go on through the Snoxhall Playing Fields. One of the Cranleigh craneries was at Vachery Pond nearby. Because the Wealden Iron Industry was based in the area it could have been an old hammer pond, a river dammed to provide power for mill wheels which would operate hammers in the old iron works, a feature of the south-east of England, but during the last century it was used simply as a feeder for the canal.

On the edge of Baynards Park is the privately owned Baynards Station. The local pub, the Thurlow Arms, was built by a former owner of Baynards Manor which is the large house at the end of the tree-lined

drive just further along. Do not follow the walker's path to Baynards Tunnel, but make sure you go left under the road bridge and through South Wood. The bank you see covered in rhododendrons marks the boundary between Surrey and West Sussex. Go through Rudgwick, past the brick works, and you come over the river Arun on an odd two-tiered bridge. This was built when a railway inspector decided, in his wisdom, that the gradient to Rudgwick Station was too steep.

The A29 straddles the railway line just after the eighteen-acre Park Street Nature Reserve. This part of the A29 used to be the Roman London to Chichester road, Stane Street, and according to local legend a bell, en route from Rome to York during the occupation, is supposed to have fallen into a piece of marshy ground nearby and been lost for ever. You are now in Slinfold, and after about half a mile the Path goes under the

OS Maps: 186, 287, 298 – but the OS maps do not show the Downs Link Path as it is on the ground. The Downs Link Guide is available from the information offices at the following councils: Surrey County Council, County Hall, Penrhyn Road, Kingston-upon-Thames, Surrey GU7 1HR. Tel: 081 546 1050. Waverley Borough Council, The Burys, Godalming, Surrey KT1 2DN. Tel: Godalming 4104. West Sussex County Council, County Hall, Chichester, West Sussex PO19 1RL. Tel: 0243 777100.

Horse-box Parking:
The Manager, Bridge House Riding School, Five Oaks Road, Slinfold. Tel: Slinfold 7901637. Mrs V. Millwood, Naldretts Farm, Naldretts Lane, Bucks Green. Tel: Rudgwick 2403.

Accommodation with stables:
Mrs A. Sheldrake, Happy Landings, The Drive, Ifold, Billingshurst, Sussex RH14 0TE. Tel: Loxwood 752199. Mr & Mrs D. Jarman, Wanbarrow Farm, Bullfinch Lane, Hurstpierpoint, Sussex BN6 9ER. Tel: 0273 834110. Miss D. Stonard, Penquite Farm, Wykehurst Lane, Ewhurst, Cranleigh, Surrey GU6 7PF. Tel: (day) Byfleet 42288, (evenings) Cranleigh 277529. Mrs A. Metson, Coverwood Farm, Ewhurst, Cranleigh, Surrey. Tel: 0306 731101. Peter Parker, Lockners Farm, Chilworth, Near Guildford, Surrey. Tel: Guildford 61987. Mrs J. Sewell, East Whipley Farm, Cranleigh, Surrey. Tel: 0483 272445. Mrs Penny Field, Old Farnhurst, Cranleigh, Surrey. Tel: 0483 274646. Mrs Ruth Harrison, Woodsomes Farm, Lynwick Street, Rudgwick, West Sussex. Tel: 0403 722383. Mrs Rosemary Attfield (Camping), Gamefield Farm, The Haven, Rudgwick, Billingshurst, Sussex. Tel: 0403 722575. Mr & Mrs P. M. Sparrow, Park Guest House, Stane Street, Slinfold, West Sussex. Tel: 0403 790723.

Vets:
B. J. Green or J. G. Peters at the Arthur Lodge Veterinary Hospital, 17 Brighton Road, Horsham, West Sussex. Tel: Horsham 52964. Lakin Keeling & Clark, the Veterinary Surgery, Gardner Road, Guildford, Surrey GU1 4PQ. Tel: 0483 504156.

Farriers:
J. Facer RSS AFCL, Crateman Farm, Cowfold, Near Horsham, Sussex. Tel: Cowfold 200. Thomas Dale AWCF Hons, Southern Cottage, Purser's Lane, Peaslake, Guildford, Surrey GU5 9SJ. Tel: Dorking 730159.

Further Help:
Julia Martin, Information Officer, West Sussex County Council, County Hall, Chichester, West Sussex PO19 1RL. Tel: 0243 777100. Mr T. Campbell, British Horse Society, 1 Wales Farm Cottage, Plumpton, near Lewes BN7 3AE. Tel: 0273 890252. Miss Jane Edwards, Secretary, Long Distance Riding Group (Downs Link), Yew Tree Cottage, Fernhill, Horley, Surrey. Tel: 0293 42351.

A264. For a while you leave the railway track to go past Weston's Farm and the village of Itchingfield. You must follow the signs carefully through Christ's Hospital school, and eventually you pick up the old railway at Itchingfield Junction.

You take a circuitous route through Southwater, and cross the A24 at the pelican crossing. The countryside is suddenly rather refreshing after unimpressive Southwater. Just before you come to Copsale you can see Copsale Court. Cowfold Church contains the well-known fifteenth-century brass of Thomas Nelond, Prior of Lewes.

On the other side of the A272 Cowfold road, and just a little further on you will see the old platforms of West Grinstead Station. Despite being damned by implication in Alan Ayckbourn's plays, West Grinstead itself is a pretty village, grouped around its church, beside the river Adur. The church has painted walls, and, unusually, the names of local farms carved into some of the pews. The village of Shipley is only a couple of miles away, where the traveller and poet Hilaire Belloc lived in the mill house from 1906 until 1953 when he died. He owned the windmill beside it which is kept open in his remembrance, as the only surviving smock mill in West Sussex. Also in the village is a twelfth-century church with Norman arches under the tower put up by the Knights Templars. John Ireland, the composer, is buried in the graveyard.

You follow the B2135 for a while, which is a fast road and perhaps the most hazardous part of the Downs Link Path, before turning off after Partridge Green. The South Downs are straight ahead of you, and the spire to your left belongs to St Hugh's Monastery. After crossing the river Adur the path comes to Henfield, which still has considerable charm, even though one has to look for it a bit amongst the new suburban development. Stretham Manor is the site of the river Adur crossing that the Romans used in the first century. Nearby is Woods Mill, headquarters of the Sussex Trust of Nature Conservation, which has a 15-acre reserve occasionally open to the public. Steyning, described in the previous chapter, lies to the west.

Bramber is home to the National Trust's Bramber Castle, a Norman fortress built in 1083 overlooking where the river Adur used to run, to guard the town for William the Conqueror. It used to be the home of the de Braose family, but was destroyed by Cromwell's roundheads. The de Braoses had an extremely bad Civil War. Knepp Castle was another of their homes, near West Grinstead, and that was destroyed at the same time. Beside that castle is Knepphill Pond, at 100 acres one of the largest in Sussex. Until the silt clogged the Adur, Bramber was one of the most influential towns on the south coast, as ships plied up that river to its port. However, in later years when William Wilberforce drove through the place, and was told where he was, he reacted: 'Bramber? really? This is the place I am Member for.' The town became a rotten borough, returning more MPs to Parliament than Manchester. Go over the verge of the Bramber and Steynings bypass, which many people don't like because there is no fence between you and the cars, and also because the route up to the bypass isn't clearly waymarked. Apart from this an exemplary job has been done by the three councils involved in the Downs Link Path: Surrey County, Sussex County and Waverley Town. You join the South Downs Way, completing the Link, near Annington Farm and St Botolphs church, known for its sixteenth-century bells.

As well as maintaining the link between the North and South Downs Way, the local councils thoroughly support it with published material, which include route maps, giving even more precise directions than Ordnance Survey. The councils' plasticated maps give a variety of circular routes off the link too, enabling riders to vary the direction and distance of their rides. This seems to be typical of the contemporary approach to providing bridleways: spreading the burden from a single track and making possible paths and tracks to suit all types of rider.

The Midlands

Reservoir in the Upper Dove valley.

The Peddar's Way

The Peddar's Way for riders follows 70 miles of a Romanized section of the prehistoric Icknield Way, from near Thetford, at Norfolk's southern border, north to Holme-next-the-Sea on The Wash. The Icknield Way was the ancient track which connected the Ridgeway with the east of England. This section of it was rebuilt by the Romans in the first century AD, and at some points the embankment they raised to carry it has been excavated. It was approved by the Countryside Commission in 1982 to become the tenth trail of its kind.

It crosses the 300 square mile Breckland of Norfolk and Suffolk, one of the least populated areas in Britain. This tract is next to the more heavily cultivated Fens, and popular amongst both birdwatchers and anglers. The 'Brecks' were the heaths farmed by prehistoric man using a technique we might today call slash-and-burn. Over the ensuing centuries the land reverted to being heath, though renowned for its sand storms. Since the 1920s the Forestry Commission has been planting austere ranks of fir here to try to keep the topsoil in Norfolk, and has recently put in a few deciduous trees as well.

The name 'Peddar's Way' is a sixteenth-century corruption of the Latin root 'Ped', because most of the traffic along it was on foot in those days. It was called the 'Pedlar's Way' on the 1845 map in the typical nineteenth-century manner of standardizing everything to make it more explicable. At certain points the horse route is kept separated from the walking route and it diverges from the original Icknield Way where necessary to avoid the odd bolshy landowner. There is still a bad stretch near Threxton,

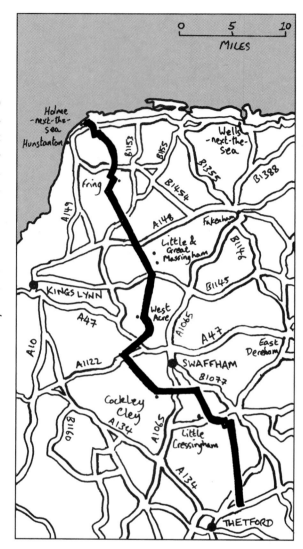

with an uncooperative farmer. The Highway Department and the Countryside Commission have not done anything about this matter so far, which shows how even named established routes are not perfect and need constant preservation and upgrading. The conscientious waymarking falls off somewhat after Fring, but one should not be too harsh on Norfolk County Council, when so few other authorities are able to publish anything as good as *The Peddar's Way – A*

Route for Horseriders as they do. The ride is easy, and the surface is sand and flint, which is not as slippery after rain as chalk. Some of the route is on metalled roads, and it is fast traffic on these roads which causes the most problems to riders. The A47, the main Swaffham to Kings Lynn Road, is also difficult to cross.

The ride begins at the railway off the A11 at Bridgham Heath. Nearby Thetford expanded considerably after the Second World War, but has managed to hold on to its heritage. The Town, which is where the Icknield Way crossed the rivers Thet and Little Ouse, has some unusual Saxon remains, dating from when it was the capital for the kings of East Anglia, as well as a number of ancient religious sites. At one stage the town held twenty churches and four monasteries. The Bishop of East Anglia was based here for the latter part of the eleventh century, and the ruined Thetford Priory is worth seeing. The author of *The Rights of Man* and *The Age of Reason*, Thomas Paine, was born here in 1737, and a statue commemorates him in White Hart Street. In the Ancient House, once the home of a Tudor merchant, there is a museum showing aspects of the development of Breckland. Outside the town is Castle Hill, which has the remains of an Iron Age settlement.

Ride north from the railway through the Forestry Commission woods around Thetford, which include Roudham Heath. They now constitute the largest forest in lowland Britain, and are criss-crossed with riding trails. Information about these can be obtained from the Commission's headquarters at Santon Downham. Much of this forest was planted on former heathland, but Bridgham Heath and Brettenham Heath have been kept extant, and are now Sites of Special Scientific Interest.

Go right for a hundred yards up the A1075 after Stonebridge. The windmill in Stonebridge was built in 1875, but abandoned 50 years later, and now looks rather naked without its sails. It was turned into a private house in 1958. Thomas Water, a little further on is owned by the Norfolk Naturalists' Trust, and is only open to members. It was once an oasis for the livestock which was herded along the Peddar's Way. Beyond it is the village of Thompson.

The area on East Wretham Heath to the west of the track is an army training ground, and is liberally scattered with unexploded shells, so don't stray away from the track at this point. The boggy and mysterious East Wretham contains places with names like Fowl Mere, and the Devil's Punchbowl. The latter has a picnic area, which rather spoils the effect. Merton Park, after the wood on the right beyond Sparrow Hill, has belonged to the de Grey family since the early fourteenth-century. The present Lord Walsingham lives at the seventeenth-century Merton Hall, which was the original setting for the *Babes in the Wood*. Those unlucky children can still be heard wailing in nearby Wayland Wood.

Go left at the Home Farm and follow this track until the B1108, which is quite a busy road. This will take you past Threxton Hill to Little Cressingham, where you could spend the night. Just nearby at Woodcock Hall are the remains of a Roman outpost, which had connections with traffic on the Peddar's Way. Turn right opposite the pub in Little Cressingham. This track leads to the quieter B1077, over the river Wissey, and by Pickenham Hall, which was built in 1903 to replace an eighteenth-century Palladian pile. The pretty flint gatehouse stands at the cross-roads by the Norman church in South Pickenham. The extraordinary shapes of the Scots pines outside the village towards Cockley Cley were caused by hedges growing out of control during World War II. The trees were first planted to stop the sandy soil from blowing away in the winds which whip across this flat land. The Iceni village at Cockley Cley, which is in the style of a settlement of 61 AD, the year of Boadicea's revolt against the Romans, was actually built in 1,971 AD. There may well have been such a place on that spot as traces of a moat and an old well show. The museum opposite, in the old forge, traces the history of the Iceni.

Oxburgh Hall, near Oxborough, is worth a detour. It is now owned by the National Trust and it is open most of the time, though the Bedingfield family for whom it was built in 1482 still live there. To look at from the outside it is one of the most imposing buildings in the county. Its gatehouse with twin octagonal towers rises 80 ft from the moat, and it isn't difficult to imagine Henry VII leading his magnificent retinue clattering over the bridge. The interior is a catalogue of the last 500 years, as each room dates from a different age.

Swaffham is another interesting place in the area. Well-known there is the tale of the pedlar of Swaffham. A pedlar called John Chapman woke up one morning in the fourteenth century having had a dream that he would find enormous wealth in London. Being somewhat impulsive he started at once on the walk to the capital along the Peddar's Way. Eventually he met an equally starry-eyed Londoner going the other way who claimed to have dreamt of treasure buried in Chapman's garden. Our hero immediately went back to Swaffham and dug under a tree, where lo and behold there was a crock of gold. He gave the whole lot to St Peter and Paul's church in the town to build the north aisle. There's a moral there.

The cross in Swaffham's triangular market was built by Horace Walpole, 4th Earl of Oxford during the eighteenth century, and is actually a rotunda. After Cockley Cley you ride along Fincham Drove, the Roman road between Smallburgh and Denver from where roads led all over the rest of the country. Just before it you have to cross the lethal A47, so take great care.

The remains of the priory at West Acre are superb, but unfortunately not open to the public. This was an Augustinian priory, built at the beginning of the twelfth century, and was the first Roman Catholic institution to give way voluntarily to Henry VIII during the dissolution of the monasteries and the reformation. Next to the old gatehouse is All Saints' church, which is mostly Perpendicular. To the east of West Acre are South Acre and Castle Acre. Castle Acre is noted for the ruins of its eleventh-century Cluniac priory, and for the castle, which was built for the 1st Earl of Surrey, William de Warenne. St James's church is a Perpendicular style building, and contains some fabulous artefacts, including a hexagonal pulpit and a high font cover. St George's church in South Acre has a grand alabaster monument of Sir Edward Barkham who was Lord Mayor of London in the early seventeenth century. After rejoining the Peddar's Way proper you pass Great Massingham and Little Massingham on the right. At this point in your journey you may encounter some rather exalted riders, as Sandringham is only a couple of miles away.

Between the A148 and the B1153 is Anmer Minque, a Bronze Age tumulus. Leaving that section of the old Roman road, the road through Fring is not easy at all. Eventually you pass the Docking Workhouse, which was built in 1836. After it you cross the old

OS Maps: 143, 144, 132.

Horse-box Parking:
Beside the track off the north side of the A11 at Bridgham Heath, which needs permission. On the forestry track opposite the Warden's house at the East Wretham Heath Nature Reserve, which also needs permission.

Commercial Riding Centres:
Miss N. R. Wheeler, Home Farm Riding Stables, Holme-next-the-Sea, Hunstanton, Norfolk PE36 6LF. Tel: 0485 25233. Mrs Bates, Stanbrook Riding Centre, Paddock Farm, Lower Road, Holme Hale, Thetford, Norfolk IP25 7EB. Tel: 0760 22125.

Accommodation with stables:
Mrs Davies, Clermont House, Little Cressingham, Norfolk. Tel: Watton 881997. Mrs Davey, Cley House, Threxton, Watton, Norfolk. Tel: Watton 882161. Mrs C. J. Eagle, 21 Stocks Green, Castle Acre, Norfolk. Mrs A. Wilkin, Lime Kiln Farm, Banham, Norfolk. Tel: Quidenham 401. Courtyard Farm, Bunkhouse Barn, Ringstead, Hunstanton, Norfolk PE36 5LQ. Tel: 0485 25369.

Vets:
Marriott Wilkinson & Skinner, The Old Golfhouse, Brandon Road, Thetford, Norfolk IP24 3ND. Tel: 0842 64244. Marriott Wilkinson & Skinner, 55a High Street, Watton, Norfolk IP25 6AB. Tel: Watton 881415.

Farriers:
F. W. Bush RSS, Pear Tree Farm, Southbrugh, Thetford, Norfolk IP25 6TE. Tel: 0362 820387. Cousins, Kings Lynn, Norfolk. Tel: Kings Lynn 840425. A. C. Riches RSS, 74 Moor Farm Cottages, Bircham, Kings Lynn, Norfolk. Tel: Syderstone 267.

Further Help:
J. M. Shaw, Director of Planning and Property, County Hall, Martineau Lane, Norwich, Norfolk NR21 2DH. Mrs Cleasby-Thompson, Blackhill House, The Arms, Little Cressingham, Norfolk. Tel: Watton 882465. Mrs C. Feakes, Reeves Hall Long Distance Riding Club, Reeves Hall, Hepworth, Diss, Norfolk IP22 2PP.

Sandringham, a hoofbeat away from the bridlepath, exercises a profound horsey influence on the area.

railway track, which was once part of the Great Eastern Railway. It was opened in 1866, and the last train rattled the Wells–Heacham line 100 years later.

The windmill at Ringstead is one of only six in Norfolk to have had six sails. Most have four. It was built in 1845, but stopped working during the 1920s. To the right is Beacon Hill which, at 160 ft, towers over this part of Norfolk.

Just down the coast, Hunstanton is one of the resorts developed by the Victorians along the Norfolk coast. It is sometimes called St Edmunds, due to the church of that name, and to differentiate it from Old Hunstanton which lies to the north, and which for nearly 1,000 years was the home of the le Strange family. The new Hunstanton has sandy beaches, and a rather drab funfair. It is unusual in that it is west-facing. If you do find yourself on the beach, look at the remarkable cliffs which have alternate red and white stripes of chalk and carstone. The lighthouse is now a private house.

It is not known exactly where the Peddar's Way proper ended, but the bridleway stops at Holme-next-the-Sea. This town is noted for the autumn migration of birds, and there are hides from which to view the phenomenon.

Dovedale, in the White Peak, haunt of Izaak Walton.

The Peak District

There are really two Peak Districts. The White Peak lies in the centre and the south, where pearly grey patches of limestone break the surface, and in the north broods the Dark Peak, where dark millstone grit forms the rock of the high moorlands. Sir John Betjeman hailed the geology as 'stone of such variety, colour and quality as is found nowhere else in England.' The Tissington and High Peak Trail start in the south, so for the purposes of this chapter let us ignore the Dark Peak and instead look at the White. There are numerous bridleways and two packs hunt the district, the Barlow and the High Peak Harriers. There are miles of open access country, and four marked trails, the Monsal, Manifold Track, High Peak and Tissington, which lie in the main on old railway lines. The first two are unsuitable, the Monsal apparently destined to return to railway use. However, parts can still be ridden.

Confusingly, the Peak District doesn't actually have any peaks as such. It was named after the hill dwellers who lived there during the seventh century, the Pecsaetans. The High Peak and Tissington trails lie roughly between 800 and 2,000 ft and aren't

Hang-gliding off Mam Tor, looking towards Hollins Cross and Lose Hill. (Glyn Satterley)

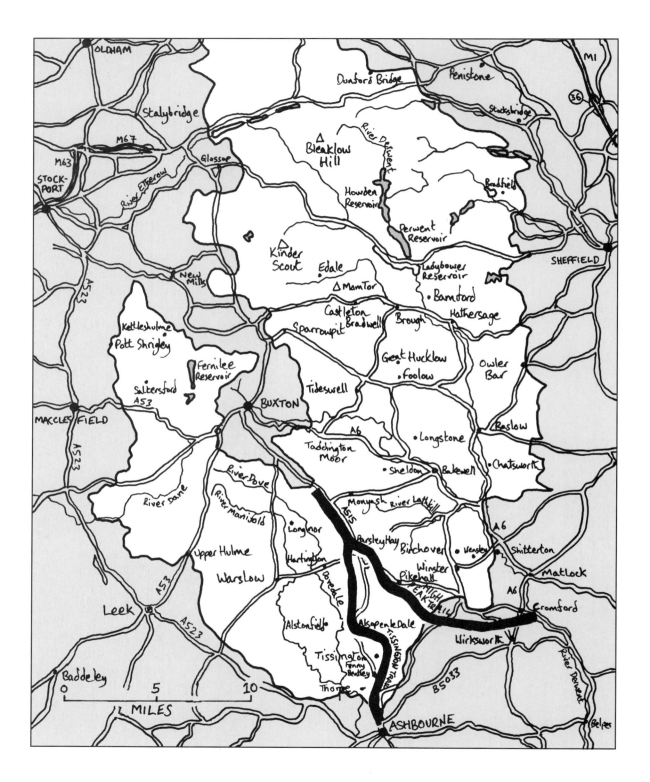

steep. The going is firm to hard and the two routes can be tackled by all breeds throughout the year except during deep snow. Together they make a weekend's good entertainment. The High Peak Trail, Cromford to Dowlow, near Buxton, and the Tissington Trail, which starts at Ashbourne and runs north to join the High Peak Trail at Parsley Hay, together comprise 30 miles of riding, shared with walkers and cyclists. They were opened in 1971 and are supervized by two full time rangers. There is strong National Park organization of riding and many other leisure activities in the Peak District. Trail riding is advertized (along with walking holidays and hang-gliding), and there is one establishment which offers a 200-mile ride along negotiated routes to the Yorkshire Dales, for extremely competent riders only.

When the 11½ mile disused railway line which forms the Tissington Trail was brought by the Peak Park Joint Planning Board there was some work to be done to it. All the disused stations on the way were demolished, and the rails and sleepers removed. The ugly, and painful, limestone chunks which remained were covered in quarry overburden and when grass was planted the track became the pleasant green it is today. The 17½ miles of the High Peak Trail, also an old railway line, was built with ash under its sleepers, so by the time it was bought by the Board in 1971 it was already grassy.

The Tissington Trail begins in Ashbourne, the gateway to the Peak. The thirteenth-century St Oswald's Church in Ashbourne dominates the skyline with its 212 ft spire, and is called the Cathedral of the Peaks. In 1645 Charles I went to a service there after he lost the Battle of Naseby. In it there is the most important piece of the town's culture,

the sculpture in white Carrera marble by Thomas Banks of five-year-old Penelope Boothby who died in 1791. There are also memorials to the important local family the Cokaynes. Ashbourne abounded with Cokaynes in the sixteenth century, and their old home, Ashbourne Hall is now the county library. The town's grammar school was founded by Sir John Cokayne in 1585 and parts of the original building are still used. Opposite that school is the home of the poet Dr John Taylor where his friend Samuel Johnson often visited him.

The Ashbourne to Buxton line was opened in August 1899. It was built by the engineer Francis Stephenson for the London & North West Railway Company. Stephenson was widely acclaimed for the Coldeaton Cutting which is 60 ft deep and three-quarters of a mile long. Although this railway was heavily used by the quarrying industry to transport the lime to be crushed at Buxton, and even supplied London with milk from Hartington at one stage, it closed to general passenger use in 1954, and was derelict by 1967.

The Tissington Trail goes near Thorpe to Fenny Bentley. St Edward's Church in Fenny Bentley has an extraordinary alabaster sculpture of Thomas Beresford, his wife, and no less than 21 children. The next town you reach is Tissington itself, which is grouped prettily around a triangular green. One of Tissington's most charming custom is well-dressing. This is the ceremony, on Ascension Day, of thanking the wells for the water they have provided over the year. It dates back to the middle of the fourteenth century, and may have pagan roots. The carvings of animals on the Norman font in Tissington's church are worth seeing. After Shaw's Farm and Newton Grange the Tissington Trail goes under the A515. It continues through Coldeaton, Biggin and

Heathcote. Hartington, to the west, has remarkable gargoyles on its church, and is a short step from Beresford Dale, that part of the River Dove extolled by Izaak Walton and his friend Charles Cotton in *The Compleat Angler*. Crossing the B5054 brings you to Parsley Hay which is where the Tissington Trail joins the High Peak Trail.

The High Peak Trail begins at High Peak Junction just beside the canal in Cromford. This town lies in the Derwent Valley, off the A6. The Jessop family had strong links with Cromford through the Butterley Company. William Jessop built the Cromford Canal, which opened in 1794. It now runs from here to Ambergate and is fed by the River Derwent at the Leadwood Pump House when the level falls too low. The pump machinery has been restored, and the Canal Society has opened it to the public. William's son Josiah constructed the Cromford and High Peak Railway Line to link it with Whaley Bridge on the Peak Forest Canal. In 1830 when it opened, the journey took a whole day. Horses pulled the train on the level sections of the line and stationary winding engines hauled it up inclines. After the decline in quarrying the line closed in 1967. The wharf shed, where goods were transferred between the canal and the railway, is now a hostel for large self catering parties.

Cromford's history really began when the father of the textile industry, Sir Richard Arkwright, built the first mechanized cotton mill in the village in 1771. He expected his work force to be frightened of the new-fangled machines and to want to destroy them, so the building which housed them was made strong enough to withstand

Packhorse Bridge across the river Wye

a siege. He also built cottages for his employees, St Mary's Church and Willesley Castle.

The High Peak Trail starts by going up the Sheep Pasture Incline, which is 1,320 yards long and steep in places. At the bottom there is a catchpit which was built after two heavy wagons broke free in 1888, sped clattering down the hill and at the bottom launched into space with airy grace clearing both the canal and the main Manchester railway, before plumetting into a field opposite. The Sheep Pasture Engine House at the top is now empty, but once held the two engines which hauled heavy goods up the incline. Further along, the Black Rocks are a well-known local landmark. Their 80 ft sheer gritstone faces have made them popular with climbers. The view from the top is startling, and in the distance you can see Ribler Castle, now a zoo, at Matlock. You cross the B5036 and the B5023 to the north of Wirksworth.

Wirksworth was the most important place on the Derbyshire lead mining map. Although the economics of that industry collapsed during the nineteenth century, the town's Moot Hall, built in 1814, still holds the Barmote lead mine court. It also has a bronze dish dating from the sixteenth century used as the area's standard measurement for lead. George Eliot set parts of her novel *Adam Bede* in the town, and the rest in Ellaston and Roston, to the south west of Ashbourne near the Tissington Trail. Wirksworth has made a huge effort to spruce itself up and not decline into depression, and in 1983 it was given a Europa Nostra award. St Mary's church has some ancient Christian carving, and the lid of a saint's coffin dating from the ninth century.

The trail passes to the south of Middleton. It is now a limestone quarry town, but was once a lead mining village. Its quarries over-

look the Via Gellia, which is not a Roman road at all. The owner of Hopton Hall, Philip Gell, built it as a pretty path through the bluebells of the woods between Cromford and Grangemill. To reach Middleton Top you have to negotiate the 708 yards of the Middleton Incline. The Middleton Top Engine House is the home of the steam winding engine built by the Butterley Company in 1829 to pull the wagons up the Middleton incline. It is open at weekends. After it you plunge into the darkness of Hopton Tunnel, which is 113 yards long, and comes out onto the Hopton Incline. This was the steepest hill a train had to climb, with a gradient of one in fourteen for 200 of its 457 yards. There will soon be bridleways connecting this part of the High Peak Trail with the new Carsington Reservoir. Nearby Harboro' Rocks are caves once lived in by Stone Age man.

The Romans never settled in the Peak District, but they did mine lead there, and Brassington, to the south, was a great centre for this industry. There is a Roman road called The Street leading from here to Buxton. The village of Brassington boasts a pretty medieval church, and houses dating back to the sixteenth century.

The High Peak Trail goes through the disused Longcliffe station. The buildings which remain include the station master's house, a warehouse, and the loading wharf for the nearby quarry. After it is Daisy Bank, and you go past Minninglow Hill. There is a disused quarry on your right. At one stage an area the size of a football pitch and two storeys thick was being quarried from the Peak District. This created employment and some startling cliffs, but also

The Wynnats Pass near Castleton. (Glyn Satterley)

unsightly detritus, and it was soon apparent that the fabric of the Peak District would fall apart. The recession of the 1970s appears to have halted the quarrying, and with Whitehall's concern for the environment today it is unlikely to pick up again to the same extent.

Gotham is really not exciting at all. However, it is from here that the *Merrie Tales of the Mad Men of Gotham* first emanated in the sixteenth century. These were stories that the loopy inhabitants of this lead-mining village were rolling cheeses down the hills to Nottingham, were trying to drown eels in the village pond, and were building a hedge around a cuckoo so that they could have its delightful song all year. It is likely that all this had been a cunning ploy to discourage King John from building a hunting lodge in the area.

After Upperhouse Farm you cross the A5012 and go under the A515. This brings you to Parsley Hay, and the Tissington Trail. The High Peak Trail leads you past Cotesfield and Sparklow next. Much of this area was summer grazing for the sheep of the local monasteries, though flocks belonging to Dunstable Priory as far away as Bedfordshire and Basingwerk Abbey in Flint were also common. The main breeds on the Peaks today are the Derbyshire Gritstone and the smaller but tougher Swaledale. The High Peak Trail ends at Hurdlow Town and Dowlow.

A view of Miller's Dale.

OS Maps: 110, 119. (Outdoor leisure 1:25000 No. 24 The White Peak)

Commercial Riding Centres:
Mr D. C. & Mrs M. E. Andrews, Northfield Farm Riding & Trekking Centre, Flash, near Buxton, Derbyshire SK17 0SW. Tel: 0298 2543. Mrs Y. I. J. Bartlett, Hopkin Farm, Tansley, Matlock, Derbyshire. Tel: Matlock 582253. M. & H. Lester, Yew Tree Farm Stables, Hazlewood, Derbyshire DE6 4AE. Tel: Derby 841364. Miss K. Riley, Moorlands Trailriding, The Mill, Winkhill, Leek, Staffordshire ST13 7PP. Tel: Waterhouses 308638. Angie Rann, Moorlands Activity Holidays, Tourist Information Centre, 1 Market Place, Leek, Staffordshire ST13 5HH. Tel: 0538 381000.

Accommodation with stables:
Mrs P. Johnson, Park Hill Farm, Cubley, near Ashbourne, Derbyshire DE6 2EZ. Tel: 0335 23321. Mrs Caroline Dale-Leech, Red House Stables (includes working carriage museum), Old Road, Darley Dale, Matlock, Derbyshire DE4 2ER. Tel: 0629 733583.

Vets:
Dr D. D. Pout, Draglow, Ashbourne Lane, Chapel-en-le-Frith, Derbyshire. Tel: 0298 813430. D. J. Bowman, The Veterinary Surgery, 66/68 Mill Lane, Macclesfield, Cheshire SK11 7NR. Tel: 0625 611526.

Farriers:
P. King RSS, The New House, Dingreave Avenue, Darley Dale, Matlock, Derby. Tel: 0629 733659. J. S. Mee RSS Hons, Pear Tree Farm, Yaldersley Lane, Bradley, Near Ashbourne, Derby. Tel: Brailsford 684.

Further Help:
A. G. Harrop, British Horse Society, County Bridleways Officer, Derbyshire, Devonshire House, Surrey Street, Glossop, Derbyshire SK13 9AJ. Mr Harry Jones, Peak National Park, Aldern House, Baselow Road, Bakewell, Derbyshire DE4 1AE. Tel: 0629 814321. Mrs A. Kellie, Secretary, Long Distance Riding Group High Peak, Shatton Hall Farm, Bramford, near Sheffield S30 2BG. Tel: 0433 20635.

The Monsal Trail crosses the river Wye on a spectacular viaduct.

The North

Wensleydale from Witton Steeps. (David Ward.)

The Yorkshire Dales

Many of the National Park's 1,200 miles of public rights of way are bridleways, marked by large blue discs. The small yellow discs are footpaths. There are long-distance routes such as the 25-mile Ingleton Ride run by the Endurance Horse and Pony Society of Great Britain which goes round the Three Peaks. However, the Three Peaks Bridleways Association is concerned that this is not an appropriate time to release information regarding long-distance rides in the Yorkshire Dales, because of the feasibility study for the proposed Pennine Bridleway.

The park is draped over the saddle of the Pennines, and the Pennine footpath slices through the middle. To the north is Cumbria and County Durham, and to the west is Lancashire. The boundary to the east is cut somewhat abruptly by the military zones near Richmond and the reservoirs at Nidderdale which feed Leeds and Bradford, and the A65 forms the southern line. Dale is the Norse word for Valley, and the park consists mostly of dales, over 50 in all, but only a few important ones. There are a number of fells over 2,000 feet, of which the most popular among walkers are the three Peaks of Whernside, Ingleborough and Pen-y-ghent. What few trees there are in the park peter out above 1,700 ft, so the views are

Good grazing at the Rawlinshaw Trekking Centre, near Austwick.

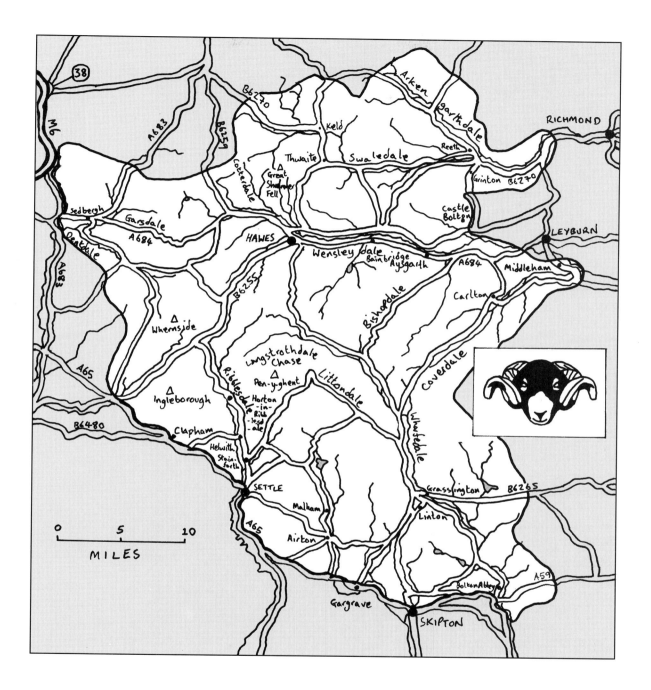

quite magnificent across the windswept grass-covered limestone.

It wasn't until the Norse came to England that man gained any sort of proper foothold in the upper dales. Then the farming became organized, and the great abbeys of Fountains, Rievaulx and Bolton all staked their claim on the pastures. These religious houses went on to become immensely rich from the sale of wool. When they were dissolved their estates were broken into small farming communities. At the end of the eighteenth century, the hated enclosure awards were being granted, and it was then that the dales' distinctive dry stone walls were built. The legacy of the nineteenth century was the extensive lead mines, and the most expensive railway of its day, with tunnels and viaducts for much of its length, from Carlisle to Settle, to transport the metal. It is now part of the main line between Carlisle and London, and subject to constant threats of closure.

The most famous character from the Dales this century has been James Herriot, though his Skeldale House surgery hasn't been included in this chapter's fact box. The popular television series *All Creatures Great and Small* has probably done more than anything to attract visitors to the Dales. Some eight million come each year, though, according to park statistics, 90% stay for less than six hours.

Starting from the north-east corner near Richmond, Reeth, where Arkengarthdale and Swaledale meet, is the home of the Swaledale Folk Museum in the building of the old Methodist Sunday School. Bridleways come from Booze Moor, Arkendarthdale Moor and Melbecks Moor to Reeth Low Moor. The church at nearby Grinton is called the Cathedral of the Dales. It is a fine Perpendicular style building where in the Middle Ages corpses from all over that part of the Dales were brought to be buried, probably along the same track which you can ride across Harkerside Moor to Castle Bolton. To the south-east is ruined Marrick Priory, a Benedictine convent of the twelfth century. The miller's house beside Arkle Beck is notable for the millstones set above the windows. Near the head of Swaledale at Keld, north of Thwaite, the cascading Kisdon Force on the river Swale is worth looking at. You are close to the Pennine Way here, which is rideable in parts. The Tan Hill Inn, by Raven Seat, is the highest pub in England at 1,732 ft. They pull a pint there with a good head – for heights.

Going west from Thwaite over Great Shunner Fell you come to Cotterdale, and beyond that Garsdale. Sedbergh, at the foot of that valley, is home to the well-known public school. It also has a fine bridge and church, and strange fells, the Howgills, above it. Their rounded shape is geologically unique. Just south is Dentdale, through which runs the River Dee. In Dent itself, there is a stone fountain commemorating the geologist Adam Sedgwick.

The three peaks, Whernside, Pen-y-ghent and Ingleborough, were created by the Craven fault. The fault's astounding scale is best appreciated from Buckhaw Brow. There is a superb ride around Scales Moor in the shadow of the north-west side of Ingleborough Hill, starting at Chapel-le-Dale. As you come off the B6255 ignore the right turn to the church, but ride on past the farm. The track is straight for about three miles along Twistleton Scars. After the camp site at Beezley, and just before the road bends left, steer your beast right through a gate up to Scar End. At Scar End you go left in the farmyard, and then right and zigzag in and out of the limestone crags up the fell. From

Looking at Pen-y-ghent from Fountain's Fell. One day it will be an official route for horses. (Glyn Satterley)

the top you can see the ridge that goes on up to the top of Whernside, and the Ribble Head viaduct. The bridleway is less obvious on Scales Moor itself, and the beautiful views are distracting to say the least, but if you continue due north-east you will come to an old railway carriage by Ellerbeck Farm. At the ford you can either go straight on and right round Ingleborough Hill even as far as Austwick, or right to arrive back at the church in Chapel-le-Dale.

Clapham sits prettily on a little beck at the foot of the other side of Ingleborough Hill from Scales Moor, just to the south. St James's church in the village has a good Perpendicular tower. Clapham has an abundance of acacia and rhododendron, and even more exotic plants at Ingleborough Hall, which was the home of the botanist Reginald Farrer, and is now a school. Nearby Gaping Gill, where water plummets into

a 378 ft hole, is a strong favourite with pot-holers. If you are riding nearby it is worth going to see if anyone is being winched down into its damp depths. From Clapham there is a bridleway through one of the most important limestone quarrying areas in the Dales, between Horton-in-Ribblesdale and Helwith. Going south down Ribblesdale along the B road, past Stainforth, you come to Settle, which has a museum of North Craven Life, as well as local man, Tot Lord's, private museum of prehistoric remains, such as rhinoceros bones found at nearby Victoria Cave. In the town is the Shambles and a building called the Folly, both dating from the seventeenth century. The latter received its name because its original owner lacked the money to complete it to his rather grandiose plans. Famous people who come from Settle include the founder of the NSPCC, Benjamin Waugh,

Dovedale, towards Weaver Hill.

and the educationalist Dr George Birkbeck. Just over the River Ribble is the public school at Giggleswick. From Langcliffe there is tiny road which eventually becomes a bridleway right up to the Pennine Way, and beyond, connecting with the network on Langstrothdale Chase. Alternatively you could go south around Malham Tarn. Malham itself is set in an amphitheatre of wild and craggy rocks. Tarn House at Malham Tarn is now owned by the National Trust, and is used by the Field Studies Council. The place inspired Charles Kingsley to write *The Water Babies*. If you want to follow the river Aire past Airton and Gargrave to go to Skipton you have to ride mainly on metalled roads.

The Craven Museum in Skipton contains relics from the local tribe, the Brigantes. At that time the Romans held all England. All England? No, for one small village held out against the invaders, the Brigantes at Ingleborough, where most of these artefacts were discovered. Skipton Castle belonged to the Clifford family for most of its life. It was built between 1300 and 1700, though an archway from the Norman Robert de Romille's original building remains. The Gatehouse has a balustrade over it inscribed with the Clifford family's optimistic motto, *Desormais*, 'Henceforth', which was put up by Lady Anne Clifford. She turned out to be the last of her line and the last occupier of the castle, and died in 1676. Skipton has a wonderfully nostalgic feel. The canal between Liverpool and Leeds runs through here, though it is more of a recreational route nowadays. The stocks still stand in Sheep Street.

To the east is Bolton Abbey, past which flows the river Wharfe. There is a pretty ride from here to Rylstone. *Strid* was the

Anglo-Saxon word for turmoil, and the place upstream from the priory where the Wharfe slips through a 12-ft ravine of limestone ledges is called the Strid. The ruins of Bolton Abbey, though perhaps not as startlingly beautiful as the abbeys of Rievaulx or Fountains, are still remarkable, with grounds leading up to the water's edge. Further up the river is crossed by stepping stones. The Abbey's nave has been repaired and roofed to be the local parish church. Nearby Bolton Hall, not the ruined one in Wensleydale, is one of the Duke of Devonshire's homes.

Upper Wharfedale Museum is at Grassington. Grassington boomed at the end of the eighteenth century with the lead mines on Grassington Moor. It has a cobbled market place, and a medieval bridge across the river Wharfe. Linton, just across the water, is dominated by Fountaine's hospital, an almshouse set up by Richard Fountaine in 1721. This village also has a pack-horse bridge and a clapperbridge.

Joining Wharfedale about half way down is the little visited Littondale, with the delightful greystone village of Arncliffe, dotted with sycamores, around a twelfth-century church. From here there are some extremely energetic bridleways over the fells to return to Wharfedale. They either end at the gorgeous village of Kettlewell, or Hubberholme at the head of the valley, which has a notable church and a 1000-year old custom attached to the vicar. Every Christmas the Hubberholme villagers troop to the George Inn where the incumbent auctions the grazing on a certain piece of land. Hubberholme is also an entrance to Langstrothdale Chase.

Bishopdale and Coverdale run parallel to each other. In Coverdale there is what little is left of Coverham Abbey. Its history has been turbulent, and has involved characters with names as romantic as Robert Fitzralf, Ralf Fitzrobert, and Helewisia de Glanville, who argued unendingly with an impossible body of Premonstratensian canons. Where Coverdale meets Wensleydale, just outside the designated National Park, are the ruins of Jervaulx Abbey, a grand, and sane, Cistercian foundation which suffered reformation like all the religious houses in the area, but which also saw the head of its last abbot removed from his shoulders for playing a part in the ill-fated Pilgrimage of Grace. It is now privately owned, and rather refreshing that it isn't quite as clipped and impeccably kept as some of the others. Ironically, it was a local man who did much to help the violent and destructive process of reformation. The 1538 Great Bible, the common people's version, was translated by Miles Coverdale.

The Forester's Arms at Carlton has a fine old English feel, with flagstones on the floor, and outside the pub kitchen a prehistoric burial mound. St Mary and St Akelda's church, to the north east of Carlton at Middleham has an extraordinary 10 ft high font cover in Perpendicular style. Middleham to Bishopsdale, and Bishopsdale to Carlton, are two rideable routes. Middleham Castle was built by the same protagonists in the Coverham Abbey story. Edward, son of Richard III 'Crookback', though that is now an unfashionable nickname, died in Middleham Castle in 1484, a year before Henry VII trounced his father at Bosworth Field, and the English crown was found hanging in a thorn bush, though that legend is equally unfashionable. Middleham Castle was eventually abandoned in 1646. These days, thoroughbreds training for the sport of kings use gallops just behind the keep. It was local monks who first made this a centre for racing.

OS Maps: 98, or the OS Leisure Guide.

Commercial Riding Centres:
Brookleigh Riding Centre, Appleby, Richmond, North Yorkshire. Tel: Darlington 718286. Catterick Garrison Army Saddle Club, Catterick, Richmond, North Yorkshire. Tel: Richmond 832521 X2661. Fremington Mill Farm, Reeth, Richmond, North Yorkshire. Tel: Richmond 84581. Grey Horse Riding Stables, Brough, Cumbria. Tel: Brough 651. Holmescales Riding Centre, Old Hutton, Kendal, Cumbria. Tel: Kendal 29388. Killington Lake Trekking Centre, Killington Reservoir House, Kendal, Cumbria. Tel: Sedbergh 20326. Mrs A. Roberts, Kilnsey Trekking Centre, Mossdale, Conistone-with-Kilnsey, Skipton, North Yorkshire BD23 5HS. Tel: 0756 752861. New Close Farm, Gammersgill, Coverdale, Leyburn, North Yorkshire. Tel: Wensleydale 40668. Newton Riding Centre, Newton Grange, Gargrave, Skipton, North Yorkshire. Tel: Gargrave 243. Rawlinshaw Trekking Centre, Austwick, Lancaster, Lancashire. Tel: Settle 3214. Swinton Riding and Trekking Centre, Home Farm, Swinton, Ripon, North Yorkshire. Tel: Ripon 89636. Messrs K. A. M. & Mrs P. C. Ancaster, Breckonbrough Riding Holiday Centre, Breckonbrough Farm, Brough Park, Richmond, North Yorkshire DL10 7PL. Tel: 0748 811629.

Accommodation with stables:
Mrs Y. Brookes, Brewery House, Brompton-on-Swale, Richmond, North Yorkshire. Tel: 0748 818117. Miss K. Egan, Cockerham Farm, Thorpe Lane, Linton, Skipton, North Yorkshire. Tel: Cracoe 380. Mr A. Hassey, Acresfield Farm, High Mere Skye, Wigglesworth BD23 4RL. Tel: 0729 4531. The YHA have facilities for horses at the following addresses, but you must book a fortnight in advance: Mr Tom Sharp, Holme House, Malham, Skipton, North Yorkshire. Tel: 0729 3352. YHA Aysgarth. Tel: 0969 3260.

Vets:
R. H. Phillips, Aylward & Phillips, 56 Market Place, Richmond, North Yorkshire DL10 4JQ. Tel: 0748 2389. Watkinson & Naish, The Veterinary Surgery, Hollin Rigg, Leyburn, North Yorkshire DL8 5HD. Tel: 0969 23107. C. C. Anderson, 95 High Street, Kirkby Stephen, Cumbria CA17 4SY. Tel: 0930 71359. Moffitt, Murray & Robinson, Thorn's Hall, Sedbergh, Cumbria, Tel: 0587 20335.

Farriers:
J. D. Jemmeson RSS, Castle House, Middleham, North Yorkshire DL8 4QD. Tel: 0969 22148. Maurice Stafford RSS, 64 High Street, Gilling West, Richmond, North Yorkshire DL10 5JW. Tel: 0748 4373.

Further Help:
John & Judith Conway, Three Peaks Bridleways Association and the Endurance Horse and Pony Society of Great Britain Lancashire Group, Rarber Top Farm, Rarber Lane, Ingleton, Carnforth, Lancashire LA6 3DW. Tel: 0468 41254. Dr Chris Wood, Information Service Officer, Yorkshire Dales National Park, Colvend, Hebden Road, Grassington, Skipton, North Yorkshire BD23 5LB. Tel: 0756 752748. Mrs R. Cope, Long Distance Riding Group, North Yorkshire Dales, 5 Exelby Close, Exelby, Bedale, North Yorkshire DL8 2JT. Tel: 0677 24894. Mrs G. M. Graham, Long Distance Riding Group North Yorkshire Dales, Middleton Quernhow, Ripon, North Yorkshire HG4 5HY. Tel: 0765 84206.

Wensleydale, named after the town of Wensley and producer of the famous cheese, is the valley of the river Ure. There is a bridleway along most of the lower part of the valley on the left bank. Holy Trinity church in Wensley has some fine pieces, such as a minutely carved rood screen, a chest reputedly containing the bones of St Agatha, from Easby Abbey, and a memorial to Dr Peter Goldsmith, who was with Nelson at his death at Trafalgar. Bolton Hall at Wensley was a seventeenth-century house destroyed by fire in 1902.

A pair of screens in Aysgarth's parish church, St Andrew's, were probably saved from Jervaulx Abbey. The well-known Yorkshire Carriage Museum at the mill by the three levels of Aysgarth Falls are also worth visiting. Fourteenth-century Bolton Castle at Castle Bolton, to the north-east, built for the 1st Lord Scrope, was where Mary Queen of Scots was kept a prisoner for six months. Much of it was taken down by Cromwell's men after the Civil War, and what remained was blown over in storms during the ensuing centuries. There is now a folk museum in its surviving great chamber.

Bainbridge was once the town which served the mighty forest of Wensleydale, and from it you can ride a couple of bag-end bridleways northwards. Every autumn and winter evening at nine o'clock a member of the Metcalfe family blows a three-ft long Cape buffalo horn on the green to bring home people lost in the forest, which no longer exists. This custom dates back at least 700 years. In the town is the museum at Low Hill, and there is a Roman road, formerly all the way from Lancaster, leading up to Semer Water to the south, from where the river Bain flows. Another local museum is the Upper Dales Folk Museum at Hawes, North of Hawes at the Green Dragon Inn is Hardrow Force, where Fossdale Beck drops 100 ft from the limestone. You can walk behind the waterfall, but horses cannot.

The Lake District

Despite a proposal for a Round Cumbria Link, there is no waymarked long distance bridleway in the Lake District. The possibility of a Lakeland Circular Ride sanctioned by the National Park Authority is awaiting a full survey of the whole route from organizations such as the British Horse Society. However, the fells are criss-crossed with such a latticework of tracks that you can ride for days. There is a lady from the Cumbria Bridleways Society who rides the bridleways for anything up to 25 days at a time! But those who don't know the area do need guidance and help, which that society can provide. This chapter will simply give background information to some of the possible rides.

The Lake District consists of three distinct parts. The north, which is made up of Skiddaw slate, is characterized by heather moorland which the poor soil like that can support. Buzzards and kestrels wheel overhead, but look out for the odd merlin. The wheatears and meadow pipits are also common. A sandpiper, a ring ouzel or a curlew is always a satisfying find. Apart from the ever-present Herdwick sheep, the most common animal is the fox. D'ye ken John Peel? He was a famous fell huntsman, immortalized by the song. But he hunted on foot, for fellhounds hunt the fox where no horse goes.

The second area of the Lake District is in the centre, and it was volcanic activity 400

Rosthwaite and Borrowdale from the path to Watendlath. (David Ward.)

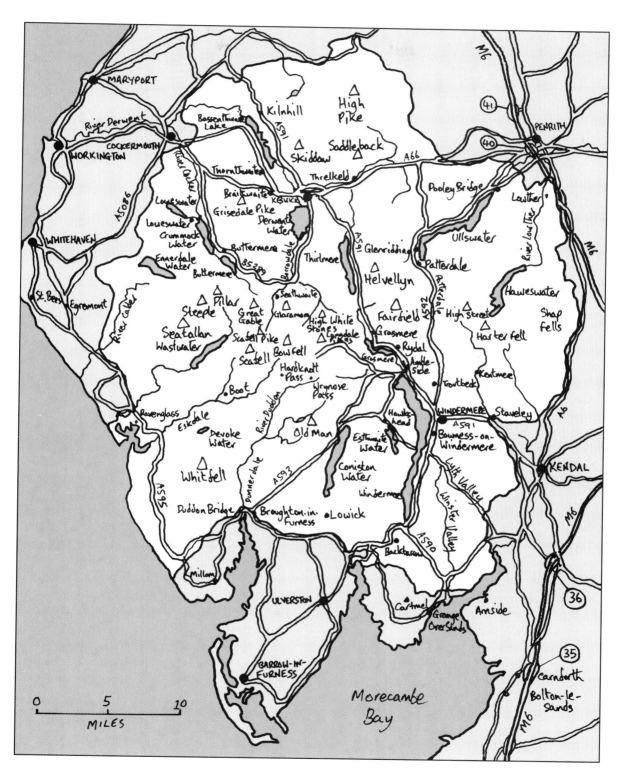

MARYPORT

River Derwent

COCKERMOUTH

WORKINGTON

Bassenthwaite Lake

A591

Kilnhill

High Pike

Saddleback

Skiddaw

A66

Threlkeld

Thornthwaite

KESWICK

Braithwaite

Grisedale Pike

Derwent Water

River Derwent

Pooley Bridge

Lowther

River Lowther

M6

41

40

PENRITH

Ullswater

Glenridding

Patterdale

Louseswater

Louseswater

Crummock Water

Buttermere

B5289

Borrowdale

Thirlmere

A591

Helvellyn

Haweswater

Ennerdale Water

WHITEHAVEN

A595

Buttermere

St. Bees

Egremont

River Calder

Pillar

Steeple

Great Gable

Seatallan

Wastwater

Scafell Pike

Scafell

Seathwaite

Glaramara

High White Stones

Ennerdale Pikes

Bow Fell

Hardknott Pass

Fairfield

Grasmere

Grasmere

Rydal

High Street

Patterdale

A592

Harter Fell

Shap Fells

Kentmere

Boot

Wrynose Pass

Amble-side

Trout beck

Ravenglass

Eskdale

Devoke Water

River Duddon

Old Man

Hawks-head

WINDERMERE

A591

Bowness-on-Windermere

Staveley

M6

KENDAL

Whitfell

Dunnerdale

A593

Esthwaite Water

Coniston Water

Windermere

Lyth Valley

Winster Valley

A595

Duddon Bridge

Broughton-in-Furness

Lowick

Backbarrow

A590

36

Millom

ULVERSTON

Cartmel

Grange Over Sands

Arnside

35

BARROW-IN-FURNESS

Morecambe Bay

Carnforth

Bolton-le-sands

M6

0 5 10
MILES

million years ago which formed the highest fells, such as Scafell Pike, the tallest of them all. The parsley fern and the silvery Alpine lady's mantle are the most obvious flora. The wheatear and meadow pippit are again the commonest birds, but there are ravens, peregrines and even the odd golden eagle. Dotterels and snow buntings are also indigenous, but rare. In general this is not suitable country for horses, but the gentler Silurian stone of the South, the third part of the Lake District, offers some lovely rides. It is a habitat for most of the Lakeland mammals, many made famous by Beatrix Potter, and one of the last outposts of the red squirrel.

The Lake District is an exhausting place to ride, though, by and large, the bridleways, which are often old pack-horse tracks, stay away from great heights. The fells are so steep that only short distances should be attempted each day. However, the saturation of breathtaking scenery on the eyes more than makes up for the brevity of the journey. It is also impossible to maintain all the bridleways, and they frequently fall into disrepair. The screes are treacherous so take great care.

There is a bridleway from Buttermere through the Scath Gap Pass to Ennerdale, and one from Crummock Water under Gale Fell to Ennerdale Water. The leader of the mutiny on the *Bounty*, Fletcher Christian, was born a few miles north of Loweswater at Moorland Close in 1764. There is nowhere to ride on Grisedale Pike, 2,593 ft, or the west side of the Derwent Fells, so if you intend to return to Keswick you are faced with either retracing your tracks, or taking the B5292 over Whinlatter Pass. This road isn't too busy except on bank holidays. Bassenthwaite Lake is in a direct line between the Solway Firth and Morecambe Bay, both famous for their migrating birds,

which can often be seen on the lake. Francis Bacon's biographer, James Spedding, lived at Mirehouse on the shores of Bassenthwaite Lake. His wide circle among the literary figures of his day include Carlyle, Tennyson and Edward Fitzgerald. There are bridleways from here all around Skiddaw, 3,053 ft, and High Pike, 2,157 ft, to Keswick in the south, and the river Caldew in the east. On Carrock Fell, above the Caldew, is a prehistoric hillfort, once visited by Charles Dickens. However, Saddleback is too steep to ride.

Keswick itself, you will quickly notice, is a centre for the tourist industry, catering for holidaymakers and hikers as well as riders. In the town's square is Greta Hall where the poet Robert Southey lived. The Fitz Park museum at Keswick has some of his original manuscripts, as well as a few from Horace Walpole, whose novel *Judith Paris* was set in Watendlath, a few miles to the south. Robert Louis Stevenson, Scott, Tennyson and Shelley have all been guests of the Royal Oak Hotel. On Derwent Water is the island where St Cuthbert's disciple, St Herbert the hermit lived. You can ride south along the river Derwent through the stunning Borrowdale valley. The 2,000 ton Bowder stone 'lying like a stranded Vessel whose hour of danger is no more' looks rather precarious perched above Borrowdale. It actually has a ladder up one side if you want to tether the horse and climb it. Further up the valley, is the village of Seathwaite (not to be confused with Seathwaite in the Duddon Valley) which competes with places in Somerset for the greatest annual rainfall in England. The graphite for the famous Keswick pencils, mainstay of the nation's primary schools, was once mined there.

From Borrowdale there are a number of bridleways to Thirlmere. Overlooking St

Only the tough can cope with High Street. (Picture courtesy of Cumbria Bridleways Society/H. C. Fell)

Climbing from Hartsop to High Street. (Picture courtesy of Bigland Hall/Lynne Potter)

John's Beck, to the north of Thirlmere, is Castle Rock, which Sir Walter Scott mentioned in his poem *The Bridal of Triermain*. Castle Rock is sometimes called the Rock of Triermain. Hellvellyn, to the east, dominates Thirlmere. There are bridleways all over it, and the views from the top are magnificent, some as far as the Scottish mountains, 60 miles away. There are many approaches to the summit, but don't attempt Striding Edge. If you want to go to Ullswater you can come down at Glenridding and ride south to Patterdale.

Below the daffodils of Gowbarrow Park on the knee of Ullswater is Lyulph's tower. Its predecessor was built by a baron called L'Ulf, though the Victorians, in their usual way, put up their own version. Just outside the town of Patterdale is the holy well where St Patrick, patron saint of Ireland, preached and baptized converts. The local church is named after him. The vale leads on until it reaches Kirkstone Pass. But that way you are faced with the steep drop to Ambleside which natives call the Struggle. There are bridleways from Goldrill Beck over Martindale on the east side of the lake to Pooley Bridge. You can also ride from Goldrill Beck over Askham Fell to Askham, near Lowther Castle, home of the annual Lowther Horse Trials. Lowther Castle, set in 3,000 acres, was lived in by the Earls of Lonsdale until 1936, and Mary Queen of Scots once stayed there. It was destroyed by a fire in 1957, and the Lonsdales now live nearby in the fourteenth-century Askham Hall. From the river Lowther there are bridleways leading over most of the fells on each side of the valley. Haweswater Beck runs into the Lowther at Bampton.

Little Langdale, valley of the river Brathay which feeds Windermere. (Glyn Satterley)

Crossing the screes at Warnscale Bottom. (Picture courtesy of Cumbria Bridleways Society/J. Buxton)

Haweswater used to be two and a half miles long, but it was lengthened to make a four and a half mile reservoir by a dam in 1940. The village of Mardale was drowned, and the ruins of the Holy Trinity Church can sometimes be seen below the surface of the water. On stormy nights you can hear its bells tolling too, or so they say. From each end of Haweswater reservoir there are bridleways leading out over the Shap fells. At Shap is the Keld chapel, owned by the National Trust. To the south of Shap fells is High Borrow Bridge, where the Duke of Cumberland's army beat Bonnie Prince Charlie's forces. You can also ride to Kentmere. Bernard Gilpin, known as the Apostle of the North, was born at Kentmere Hall in 1517. Just to the west following the long scarp between Penrith and Troutbeck is the Roman road known as High Street, run-ning over the fell of the same name, 2,718 ft at its highest, which is mostly bridleway and one of the longest continuous stretches in the Lake District. From Kentmere you can ride to Troutbeck, home of John Peel, across the 1,475 ft Garburn Pass. The beck itself leads down to Lake Windermere, and you can ride from Troutbeck, the village, to Ambleside.

At 10½ miles long, Windermere is the largest lake in England. It has 14 islands, and Arthur Ransome set his children's adventure story, *Swallows and Amazons*, partly on this lake, and partly on Coniston. One of the islands, Belle Isle, is privately owned by the Philipson family. Their strange circular house is now, somewhat reluctantly, open to the public. Ambleside is one of the biggest Lakeland resorts, and is a centre for walkers and climbers. The Ambleside area is also renowned for its literary associations. As well as the omnipresent Wordsworth family, Keats and Coleridge stayed for a while, as did Mrs Humphrey Ward and de Quincey. De Quincey lived at Dove Cottage in Grasmere for more than a quarter of a century after Wordsworth left it in 1808. He previously lived at Nab Cottage under Nab Star, and when he left that, Hartley Coleridge, Wordsworth's greatest friend, moved in. The Knoll, towards Keswick, was where Harriet Martineau lived, and she was visited by both Charlotte Brontë and George Eliot. Matthew Arnold's father, the famous headmaster of Rugby School Dr Thomas Arnold spent his summer hols at Fox Howe, beside the river Rothay.

The town of Windermere used to be called Birthwaite, but the coming of the railway in 1847 opened it up as a resort, and the local corporation decided that the place needed a change of image. It is even more accessible from the rest of England now, so used extensively as a base for touring the Lake District. Between Windermere and Staverley there are bridleways over the gently undulating countryside of Hugill, affording spectacular views of the fells to the north.

There isn't much riding in the Lyth Valley or the Winster Valley, but north and west of Newby Bridge at the foot of Windermere are the Furness Fells with bridleways as far as Lowick and beyond to Woodland Fell. Lowick Hall was the home of Arthur Ransome. North of the Furness Fells is the Grizedale Forest. Both the fells and the forest are crossed by several bridleways, excellent riding which will lead you to Esthwaite Water.

Seventeenth-century Hill Top Farm, at Near Sawrey, is where Beatrix Potter lived, wrote and farmed. When she died in 1943 she left it to the National Trust, and it has

The Vale of Eden. (Picture courtesy of Cumbria Bridleways Society/J. Buxton)

been kept extant since then. There is also an exhibition of her paintings and illustrations in Hawkshead, at the offices of her husband, William Heelis, who was a solicitor. Another National Trust property in Hawkshead is the courthouse, which is all that is left of the manorial buildings in the town, once owned by Furness Abbey. It is now a museum.

Wray Castle, north-east of the lake, is an early Victorian House, given with its 64 acres of grounds to the National Trust by Sir Noton and Lady Barclay in 1929. Only the grounds are open to the public, Canon Rawnsley, once the vicar of Wray, was one of the founders of the National Trust.

In 1516 Edwin Sandys, later Archbishop of York, was born at Esthwaite Hall. He founded the grammar school in Hawkshead where Wordsworth went to school amongst 'a race of real children; not too wise too learned or too good'. It is a museum now, and one of the main exhibits is the desk on which the young Wordsworth inscribed his name with a pen knife. There are rides from Hawkshead over to the head of Windermere, and you can ride all round the famous beauty spot Tarn Hows.

Coniston, the former copper mining town, is to the west. It has a museum dedicated to the life of Ruskin, and in the churchyard there is a carved cross commemorating him. He lived in Brantwood, overlooking the lake. Coniston Water was where Donald Campbell was killed in 1967 while attempting a new water-speed record. The more sedate Steam Yacht Gondola, owned by the National Trust, cruises up and down the lake. It was built in 1859 and oozes Victorian resort opulence. Above the village of Coniston there is good riding on the lower slopes of the Old Man of Coniston as far as Torver, Little Langdale and Elterwater. You will be riding along old slate mining tracks, and may wish to deviate to inspect some of these sites, but be careful. Elterwater is still quite a slate mining area, though not as great as it was. The river Brathay flows out of this brief lake and the waterfall, Skelwith Force before Skelwith Bridge, is worth seeing. Over Loughrigg Fell is Rydal Water. Wordsworth lived at Rydal Mount for 37 years. Grasmere is to the west where the poet lies buried in St Oswald's Church, which he described in his poem *The Excursion*:

> Green is the churchyard, beautiful and green,
> Ridge rising gently by the side of ridge,
> A heaving surface, almost wholly free
> From interruption of sepulchral stones,
> And mantled o'er with aboriginal turf
> And everlasting flowers.

Little Langdale, where the landscape is etched with old slate mining tracks.

His headstone is most unostentatious. He also lived in the town at Dove Cottage between 1799 and 1808, and this is now open to the public.

North and west of here are the Borrowdale Volcanics, the magnificent buttresses of Great Gable and Scafell, central Lake District proper. It is often too steep for horses, but there are bridleways wending their way in and out of the fells. For those who enjoy the climb there is a packhorse road up mighty Fairfield, at 2,863 ft Grisedale Tarn is on Fairfield. It was here that Wordsworth said goodbye to his sea-faring brother for the last time before John was drowned. He wrote an elegy, part of which Canon Rawnsley had carved on a rock at the spot, near the tarn's outlet. Ullscarf, 2,370 ft, is just across valley of Raise Beck and the A591, but bridleways peter out towards Watendlath Fell. The scarp of Greenup Edge which takes in High White Stones, 2,414 ft, is crossed by a bridleway, 2,560 ft, as is Great Gable, 2,949 ft, so-called for its resemblance to the gable end of a house, and they all go as far as Wastwater. Less bleak, you could turn south and ride into Great Langdale, hailed by Wordsworth: 'a Vale which should on no account be missed by him who has a true enjoyment of grand separate Forms composing a sublime Unity, austere but reconciled and rendered attractive to the affections by the deep serenity that is spread over every thing.'

Wrynose Pass, where the old counties of Lancashire, Cumberland and Westmorland used to meet at the Three Shires Stone, is again too steep to consider, but there are bridleways leading from Hardknott Pass in all directions. Nearby Hardknott Castle was a Roman fort. The river Duddon rises at Wrynose. On the valley floor it is crossed by Birk's Bridge. This is a startlingly pretty

Luckily these riders on High Street had compass and maps. (Picture courtesy of Bigland Hall/Lynne Potter)

part of the river, which is crystal clear for most of its length, as the bright colours of the rocks which form a short chasm just here shine through the water. Wordsworth called the river's valley 'some of the most romantic scenery in these mountains', and he was a man who didn't use the word 'romantic' lightly. His poem *River Duddon* runs to 34 verses. These days local industry takes an awful lot of water out of the Duddon further down, which has all but destroyed it.

The first village is Seathwaite, with the church where the famous Lakeland vicar Robert Walker was pastor. 'Wonderful' Walker was born the youngest of 12 children, and devoted 66 years of his life to his parish. The Duddon trips down here through Dunnerdale. The farmer at Hall Dunnerdale breeds some of the best cattle in the Lake District, and frequent winners at the Lancaster show, so look out for them. Around Ulpha there are rides over Dunnerdale fells, and from above Ulpha over Whitfell towards Ravenglass. The seven miles of the Ravenglass and Eskdale Railway runs up this valley to the terminus at Dalegarth. The railway is known as Ratty, because it was built in the 1870s by a Mr Ratcliffe to bring the iron ore down from mines at Boot. Dalegarth Hall, which has sixteenth-century origins, was owned by the Stanley family, and on their estate is a magnificent waterfall. Stanley Ghyll.

The River Esk is quite a good salmon river, so after a spate stop and look for them on the bridges. You might see the fishing writer Hugh Falkus casting along some of these stretches. It is probably worth avoiding Sellafield nuclear power station, just up the coast, so take the track from Eskdale to Devoke Water or Wastwater.

Bridleway from Coniston linking with the Walna Scar road. (Picture courtesy of Bigland Hall/Lynne Potter)

Scafell Pike, highest mountain in England, and Scafell are too much for horses, though they are popular with climbers. The churchyard in the village of Wasdale Head holds the graves of many climbers, dating back to the 1880s when the sport began there.

There are bridleways from Wastwater through the Copeland Forest to Ennerdale. Wordsworth again:

You see yon precipice: – it wears the shape
Of a vast building made of crags;
And in the midst is one particular rock
That rises like a column from the vale,
Whence by our shepherds it is called,
THE PILLAR.

Ennerdale was an iron ore mining area during the Roman occupation. The churchyard was where Wordsworth set much of his poem *Brothers*. There are tracks from Ennerdale Water to Crummock Water and Loweswater over Loweswater Fell, which will bring you back into Buttermere.

This chapter doesn't recommend any single lakeland route. However, it does list some of the more satisfying areas in which to ride. If you don't enjoy roadwork and you can box your horse on, you will be spared a lot of tarmac. But bear in mind that many of the roads are difficult enough to negotiate by car, let alone a trailer as well.

OS Maps: 89, 90, 96, 97 (or the OS Lake District Tourist Map).

Commercial Riding Centres:
Mr R. J. Bigland, Bigland Hall Riding Centre, Backbarrow, Newby Bridge, Cumbria LA12 8PD. Tel: 0539 531728. Christine Dand, The Claife and Grizedale Riding Centre, Sawrey Knotts, Far Sawrey, near Ambleside, Cumbria LA22 0LG. Tel: 0966 22105. Mr & Mrs P. Jones, Holmescales Riding Centre, Old Hutton, near Kendal, Cumbria LA8 0NB. Tel: 0539 729388. Mr & Mrs Taylforth, Side Farm Trekking Centre, Side Farm, Patterdale, Penrith, Cumbria CA11 0NP. Tel: 0853 2337. Mrs W. M. Oakden, Wynlass Beck Stables, Lakeland Equestrian Enterprises, Wynlass Beck, Windermere, Cumbria LA23 1EU. Tel: 0966 23811.

Accommodation with stables:
Mrs Park, Low Sizergh Farm, Helsington, near Kendal, Cumbria LA8 8AE. Tel: 0448 60426. Mrs C. Ford, Robin Hood House and Equestrian Centre, Bassenthwaite, Keswick, Cumbria. Tel: Bassenthwaite Lake 296. Mrs Townson, Tarnside Farm, Crosthwaite, near Windermere, Cumbria. Tel: Crosthwaite 288. Lt. Col. T. J. C. Washington, Dacre Lodge, Penrith, Cumbria CA11 0HH. Tel: 0853 6221. Mrs H. Watson, 2 Woodend Villas, Tebay, Penrith, Cumbria. Tel: Orton 363. The YHA have facilities for horses at the following addresses, but you must book a fortnight in advance: YHA Baldersdale. Tel: 0833 50629. Mr R. Folder, Wilkinsyke Farm, Buttermere, Cockermouth, Cumbria. Tel: 0596 85237. Mr E. M. Wilson, Town End, Haltcliffe, Hesket Newmarket, Wigton, Cumbria. Tel: 0699 8638. Mrs Johnson, Spoon Hall, Coniston, Cumbria. Tel: 0539 441391/441674. YHA Dentdale. Tel: 0587 5251. Mrs N. Richardson, Ghyll House, Dufton, Appleby, Cumbria. Tel: 0768 351437. Mr Noel Hodgson, Bayesbrown Farm, Great Langdale, Ambleside, Cumbria. Tel: 0966 7620. Mr R. Orrell, High Gillerthwaite, Ennerdale, Cleator, Cumbria. Tel: 0946 861673. YHA Eskdale. Tel: 0940 3219. Cock and Dolphin Hotel, Milnthorpe Road, Kendal, Cumbria. Tel: 0539 28268. Mr Pascal Zalkind (Calvert Trust), Dairy Cottage, Old Windebrowe, Keswick, Cumbria. Tel: 0596 74395. Mr G. M. Robinson, Trainriggs Farm, Kirkby Stephen, Cumbria. Tel: 0768 371466. Mr Stanley Jackson, Nook Farm, Rosthwaite, Keswick, Cumbria. Tel: 0596 84691. YHA Patterdale. Tel: 0853 2441. YHA Stainforth. Tel: 0729 23577. Mr J. Hodgson, Stybeck Farm, Thirlmere, Keswick, Cumbria. Tel: 0596 73232. Mr A. J. Lancaster, Wood How Farm, Wasdale, Seascale, Cumbria. Tel: 0940 6246. Mr R. M. Simpson, High Fold Farm, Troutbeck, Windermere, Cumbria. Tel: 0539 432200.

Vets:
Geary, Proctor & Dixon, 173 Highgate, Kendal, Cumbria LA9 4EN. Tel: 0539 21344. W. B. Mavir, 26 Sullart Street, Cockermouth, Cumbria CA13 0EB. Tel: 0900 823119.

Farriers:
Godfrey Ernest Oliver DWCF, Ellersyde Farm, Gaisgill, Penrith, Cumbria CA10 3UA. Tel: 0587 4235. Joseph Nicholas Pigney, 38 Holme Riggs Avenue, Penrith, Cumbria. Tel: Penrith 63549.

Further Help:
Mrs T. P. Fell, Cumbria Bridleways Society, White Gates, Backbarrow, Ulverston, Cumbria LA12 8PA. Tel: 0539 531459. Dave Thomas, Cumbria National Park Visitor Centre, Brockhole, Cumbria LA23 1LJ. Tel: 0966 26601. Mr T. Pettitt, Secretary Long Distance Riding Group Cumbria, 6 Mason Street, Workington, Cumbria.

Crummock Water, seen from the Thackthwaite road. (Picture courtesy of Cumbria Bridleways Society/J. Jepson)

Leading down to Eskdale. (Picture courtesy of Cumbria Bridleways Society/J. Jepson)

Northumberland

The Northumberland National Park consists of 398 square miles of rich border history, woven into heather moorland and lonely farmsteads, bleak forests and tree-sheltered valleys. From the Cheviots in the north to Hadrian's Wall in the south, the local authorities offer great support to all visitors, especially riders. On the park's western borders lies the Kielder Water, the largest reservoir in Western Europe, and the centrepiece of Britain's biggest forest. The planning for the Kielder Forest began in 1922. The planners chose the 125,000 acres which included the forests of Falstone, Wark and original parts of Kielder on which to base their grand scheme. After the first plantations four years later, they were able to buy land from the Duchy of Northumberland.

A group of riders on Clennel Street during a week's tour from Kidlandee Trail Riding. The Scottish border is on the skyline.

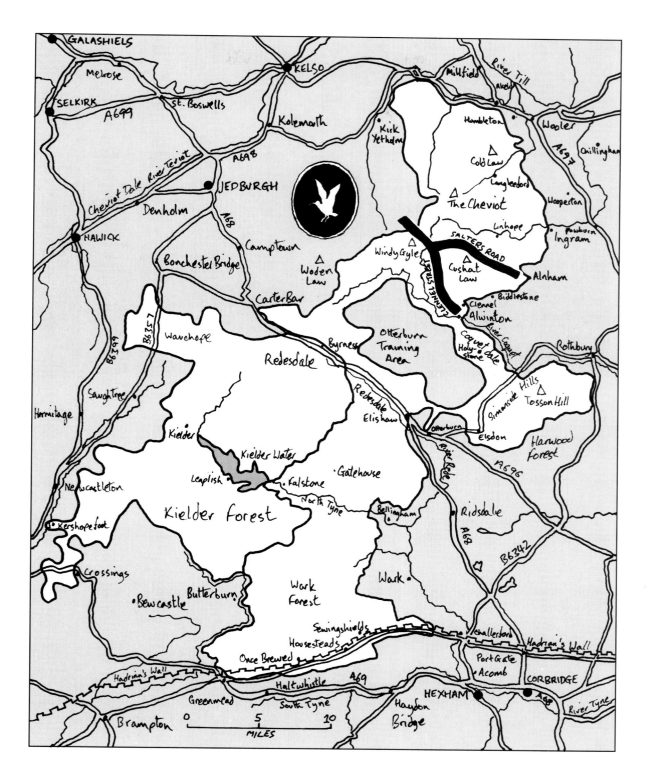

The river Coquet and beautiful undisturbed country. (Glyn Satterley.)

The forest currently stands at 200 square miles, and since this woodland was started in 1926 200 million trees have been put down.

The Northumberland National Park was created in 1955. It is the wildest upland country of England's most northerly county, and like the Kielder Forest is crossed by one of the most vigorous footpaths, the Pennine Way. The park extends from Hadrian's Wall in the south along the line of the Cheviot Hills to the border with Scotland. It has five quite distinct areas. Hadrian's Wall is one, with its links with Roman Britain, and the pastoral valleys of the North Tyne and the Rede are another two. Beyond the Army's Otterburn Training Area is Coquetdale, which curves round the Simonside Hills, and, the largest area, the Cheviots themselves.

The scenery is made up of the dull moorland grasses and heather, studded with granite outcrops and patches of sandstone. The place has a bleak feeling. The odd villages that have survived the almost continual onslaught of the Scots' raiding parties, up until James I of England, cling precariously to a lonely life amongst the hills. The skylark and the sheep are the only company. This is in stark contrast with the woods of Kielder. Most of the trees are conifers, the mainstay of the Forestry Commission, and most of those the tall, slim and conical-shaped Sitka spruce, which can survive arctic conditions. It also suits the sort of damp peat earth of the area. About a sixth of the trees are Norway spruce, the Christmas tree, but they are found mostly in the lowland areas. Knowing your trees can often help you avoid sticky places during your ride. The Scots

Sheep grazing the thin grass of the Cheviots.

The animals enjoy lunch at the head of the Coquet valley, actually on Dere Street, during a week long Kidlandee trail ride.

pine is predominant on well drained ground, along with the occasional lighter green flash of the Japanese larch, whereas the Lodgepole pine prefers it almost marshy.

Because of the wind in the Kielder Forest, the trees always look a trifle messy. However it has been found that with the land above 750 ft it is better not to thin them as would normally be done, but let them stay where they have leant or fallen to create a natural wind break. The evergreen trees are felled aged between 40 and 50 years, when they have grown to a height of up to 70 ft. Every year 700,000 trees are sent to be pulped for paper or chipboard, or used as timber beams, and 50,000 Christmas trees are topped from the Norway spruces. By the end of the century these numbers will have trebled. None of these considerations affect the Northumberland National Park. Before the Iron Age, only the valleys and the lower slopes of the Simonside Hills were inhabited, by Mesolithic hunters, and then Beaker immigrants from Europe. The Celts brought an end to the Bronze Age, and built their pallisaded settlements on hills from which they farmed their local areas. The next great culture shock was the coming of the Romans. They reached the area in about 80 AD and built a road between Carlisle and Corbridge, both of which had major forts. In 120 AD the Emperor Hadrian initiated the building of the famous wall, with forts along its route, and mile castles between the forts. Vercovivium, at Housesteads in the park, was the largest of these forts and garrisoned 1,000 men. It is spectacularly situated, and must have been an imposing building in its day.

The Romans declined and fell in the fifth century, and for 300 years Northumbria lacked organization. The Britons built defensive hillforts, often with stone stolen from the crumbling wall. In the eighth century it became more of an identifiable kingdom, but constant invasion by Vikings and Scots meant that the Northumbrians had to seek help from the south. The kingdom became an earldom in the tenth century, and from the twelfth century was run for 200 years by the Norman family de Umfraville. The hills in the northern part of the park were used as grazing by a Cistercian monastery near Morpeth. The period from 1296, when Edward I declared war on Scotland, until the Act of Union in 1603 saw havoc in the area. Many of the villages were abandoned as people fled the hungry armies travelling to or from battles, and all over the hills and dales were built the distinctive Pele houses which were lived in by the lesser gentry. The great families constructed towers, and the smallest home fortification, used mostly in outlying farms, was the bastle. In an effort to maintain some order, Edward I instituted Wardens of the Marches.

The return to sheep farming in the eighteenth century brought dry stone walls on the hills, and hedgerows in the dales. The odd circular holding pens are called stells. The two sorts of sheep found in the park, the Cheviot and the Scottish Blackface, can be impounded in these stells if the farmer is any good with his dogs. There are a quarter of a million sheep in the park, and they form a most vital mainstay of the local economy. The Otterburn Shell Firing Range is used throughout the year, but is silent during the lambing season. It is important not to stray onto the range at any time.

The Park Authority prefers you to go riding with a commercial trekking centre, and there are a number to choose from, providing all degrees of pain and pleasure on horseback, from dry, comfortable and easy, to long, wet and rewarding. However, there are sizeable bridleways in both the park and the forest which you can ride yourself. These are part of a plan for a Northumberland Long-Distance Route linking the northern parts of the park with the Kielder Forest on the park's western border. This is being devised by the Forestry Commission in consultation with the British Horse Society, the National Park authority and the army, whose zone sits in the centre of the park like the yoke of a fried egg. The proposed circuit will run through Coquetdale southwards, turning west through Bellingham, round Kielder Water, and north via an already established loop in Kielder Forest.

The Kielder Forest Route, which can be ridden now, is a fifteen mile circular track off the A68, just north of Hadrian's Wall. It takes in some of the Border Forest Park's most impressive scenery with views south over Kielder. The spectacular countryside of west Northumberland is the least populated part of England, which is why so much effort is being put into opening it up to guided routes. The Kielder Forest Route starts at Blakehopeburnhaugh, and is clearly waymarked with a horseshoe symbol. The Forestry Commission has also designated 5,000 acres around the reservoir a 'working circle' of forestry. This is an area of woodland set aside for hardwoods and other deciduous trees in order to make the water more attractive. Original features, such as the 200-year-old avenue of beeches at Leaplish, have been incorporated into this Arcadian landscape. Kielder Castle, at one end of the reservoir, was built in 1775 by the Duke of Northumberland. It was ostensibly a shooting lodge, but soon became the venue for gratuitous debauchery instead.

If you resist the trekking centres' organized rides, the route to choose in the Northumberland National Park follows the flint tracks of the Salter's Road and Clennel Street. This takes you 30 miles from Alnham on the river Aln, over the border and the Pennine Way on the Cheviot Hills to Cocklawfoot, and then back to Alwinton where the river Alwin joins the Coquet. This ride is difficult in parts, not well-signed, and doesn't have much in the way of stabling and accommodation. However, many farmhouses will stable horses in the summer when their livestock is out. An Ordnance Survey map and a compass are vital on this ride. Most horses should be able to cope with the work, though obviously the Fells and Dales breeds are the best. The route can be boggy, especially in winter, and the Salter's Road fords a few streams.

The Salter's Road was the main drove road transporting salt between England and Scotland. During the drove road boom in the eighteenth century it was one of the ways cattle were brought from Scotland to be sold in England. It begins at Alnham, which is a hamlet today. Alnham used to have its own castle which commanded this route, but that was destroyed in 1532. It still has a Pele tower to protect the locals from raiders from across the border. The hills around are full of Iron Age settlements and hillforts. The little church, St Michael and All Angels, was

Hadrian's Wall near Housesteads. (Glyn Satterley)

saved from almost certain decay in the 1960s. It has twelfth-century origins, and a monument to an impatient stonemason. Whoever carved the gushing memorial to George Adder grew bored of the endless scroll of achievements he had to chip into the stone, so he stopped abruptly with the words 'and so forth'.

You set off from the church and head for Shank House, by a small fir plantation. After it is Shank Burn, and then you cross Little Dod. Shill Moor is on the right, and you continue over High Bleakhope. You go parallel to Clay Burn and cross Usway Burn above a little Waterfall. The border is at Russell's Cairn on 2,036 ft Windy Ghyle. The Cairn is named after Francis, Lord Russell, who was murdered by Scots in 1585. The Pennine Way passes this point.

Cocklawfoot is the first place you come to in Scotland, but many people simply turn around at the border and join Clennel Street. This Roman road was one of the paths out of the Roman empire, into a treacherous land. It is not quite as difficult a surface to ride as the Salter's Road. You cross Usway Burn again, and then go through the Kidland Forest for some miles. Finally you come out at Alwinton, having followed parallel to the river Alwyn for a while. The river Coquet which the Alwyn joins is a good salmon river, and people have also found cornelians and agates in its bed, though splashing around in it looking for them will not endear you to local anglers.

The Rose & Thistle Inn at Alwinton was where the English and Scottish Wardens of the Middlemarch used to meet. There they held court over the border area. Sir Walter Scott also stayed at that pub whilst writing *Rob Roy*. St Michael's church is interesting in that it is on two levels. To go from the chancel to the nave you have to descend ten steps. It also has a superb old horse-drawn hearse garaged outside, purchased by the parish in 1830.

Commercial riding centres offer three-day rides, and a route along the coast is being negotiated. The Countryside Commission is also thinking of using Hadrian's Wall as a basis for a National Trail.

OS Maps: 80, 81.

Horse-box Parking:
Blakehopeburnhaugh, for Kielder Forest.

Commercial Riding Centres:
Charles and Elspeth Davison, Kidlandee Trail Riding, Harbottle, Morpeth, Northumbria. Tel: 0669 50254. T. Clubley, Whitton Farm House Hotel, Rothbury, Northumbria NE65 7RL. Tel: 0669 20811/20895. Donald Macleod, Brownrigg Leisure, Brownrigg, Bellingham, Northumbria NE48 2HR. Tel: 0434 220210/220272. Mr & Mrs R. Jeffreys, Kimmerston Riding Centre, Kimmerston, Wooler, Northumbria NE71 6JH. Tel: 0668 6283. Mr R. Philipson (Kielder Forest), Sinderhope Pony Trekking Centre, High Sinderhope, Allenheads. Tel: 0434 685266.

Accommodation with stables:
Mr & Mrs Coffee, (Kielder Forest), Ravenshill, Kielder, Hexham, Northumbria. Mrs A. Nichol, Hetherton, Work, Hexham, Northumbria. Tel: 0660 30260.

Vets:
Paul Freeman, Simonside Veterinary Centre, High Street, Rothbury, Northumbria. Tel: 0669 20638. Ewing & Lomax, 29 Ryecroft Way, Wooler, Northumbria NE71 6DY.

Tel: 0668 81323. Alan Clark, Clark, Malone & Young, Waggonway Road, Alnwick, Northumbria. Tel: 0665 602071. G. W. Harris MRCVS (Kielder Forest), Norwood House, St Helen's Street, Corbridge, Northumbria NE45 5BE. Tel: 0434 712033.

Farriers:
Francis Joseph Baty AFCL, Tyne Mills, Hexham, Northumbria. Tel: 0434 3078. T. Wilson RSS, 11 Burnhouse Road, Wooler, Northumbria NE71 6BJ. Tel: 0668 81744. J. W. Moorhead RSS, Smithy Cottage, Chatton, Alnwick, Northumbria. Tel: Chatton 207. Simon Heslop (Kielder Forest), 2 Wilson Cottages, Henshaw, Barton Mill, Northumbria. Tel: 0434 84354.

Further help:
Patrick Whitehead, British Horse Society County Bridleways Officer Northumbria, 9 Ploverfield Close, Ashington, Northumbria NE63 8LX. Tel: 0670 854238. J. F. Ogilvie, Management Office, Forestry Commission, Kielder Forest District, Eals Burn, Bellingham, Hexham Northumbria NE48 2AJ. Tel: 0660 20242/20243. Tony Hopkins, Northumberland National Park, Eastburn, South Park, Hexham, Northumbria NE46 1BS. Tel: 0434 605555.

Scotland

Loch of the Lowes, near Selkirk. (J. C. Ticehurst)

Dere Street

Over the border into Scotland there are no public rights of way and no law of trespass. Traditional usage determines whether a particular path may be used by, say, riders as well as walkers. This is not to say that there are no fences or barbed wire, but generally the landowners are amenable to riding on their land, especially if approached first. There are organizations such as Highland Horseback, in the north of Scotland, which claim to provide the longest trail tride in Britain, 200 miles in ten days, with all accommodation and facilities pre-arranged. Their route is from Aberdeenshire in the Eastern Highlands to the Atlantic coast of Wester Rosse. However, the Borders are historically Scotland's horse country. Dere Street follows the steps of the Romans under Agricola in his first invasion of Scotland. The bridleway won't take more than a day to ride.

One commercial establishment based in Jedburgh conducts out-and-back rides of 25 to 30 miles a day, using that part of Dere Street which is most clearly defined. Their rides down to the border then use other droves or Roman tracks, picking up the Pennine Way where that lies in Scotland, and back in a large circle. There is a great deal of riding possible in the 400 square miles of the Cheviots, though some areas, including the highest points, are extremely difficult. It is possible that the Northumberland Long Distance Route, when established, will link up with Dere Street where it meets the border of Chew Green, which was once an important Roman military post. The original Dere Street ran from York to the Tyne, and then on to Melrose.

Melrose, with its famous Abbey is the Dere Street bridleway's starting point. This little town on the river Tweed is where Sir Walter Scott lived and wrote most of his works, and the landscape's influence on his novels and poems was profound. The extraordinary house he built, Abbotsford, with its hotch-potch of styles directly lifted from places such as Linlithgow Palace and Melrose Abbey, became so expensive that eventually his creditors decided to write off their investments in recognition of his great literary works. To persuade a band of Scotsmen to do that takes real genius. Melrose Abbey was a Cistercian foundation, given in 1136 to David I of Scotland. It was first ruined during the Border Wars, but it was at the reformation that the English, under the Earl of Hertford, finished it off. The nave and choir that remain mark the last resting place of the heart of Robert the Bruce. That story began with Sir James Douglas, who had volunteered to take the great Scottish King's vital organ to bury in the Holy Land. However, in Spain on his journey he was cornered in battle with the Moors, who at the time held much of Iberia. In a last act of desperation he threw it at the advancing hordes with the cry, 'Go first, brave heart'. Douglas was killed, but his mission returned with his troops to Scotland, to lie in Melrose Abbey. Using Buccleuch money Sir Walter Scott oversaw the Abbey's restoration during the nineteenth century, and its presentation to the Scottish nation. Melrose town also has a railway museum and a vintage motor car collection.

The bridleway goes past the magical Eildon Hills with their prehistoric hillfort. It is from these three hills, blasted from one larger mound to impress the devil by the necromancer Michael Scott, that King Arthur and his knights will one day come in

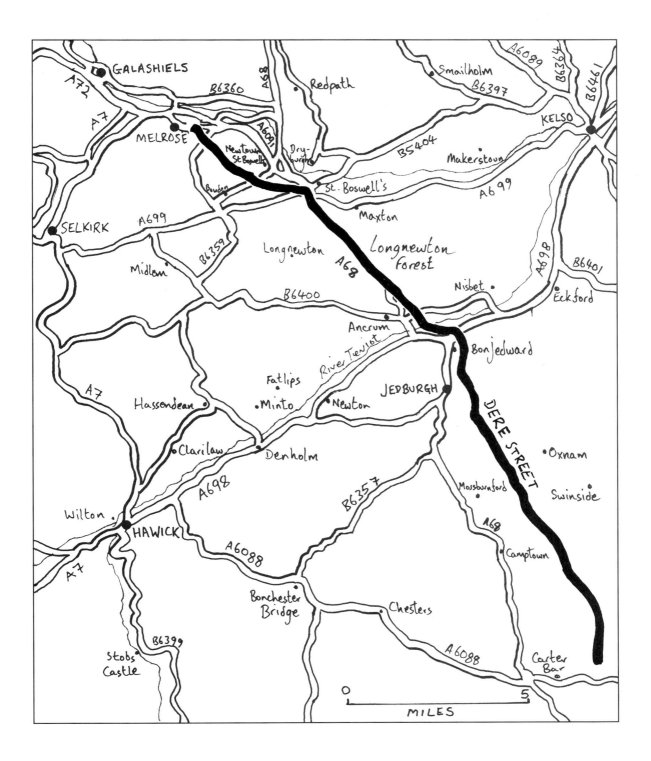

The Tweed near Dryburgh Abbey

Britain's hour of need. *Hic Iacet Arturus Rex Quondam Rexque Futurus*. Also on the hills the Tree Stone in Rhymer's Glen, where Huntly Burn descends through the trees, is where Thomas the Rhymer entered Fairyland for a seven-year stint with the Queen of the Fairies. Thomas the Rhymer, also known as Thomas of Ercildoune, was a mysterious fifteenth-century seer and poet who lived at Earlston Tower, which lies in ruins to the south. If you manage to cross the hills without Titania falling in love with you, (or on past form more probably your horse) you cross the B6398 and leave the town of Newton St Boswells to your left, which has the headquarters of the Borders Regional Council. Go over Bowden Burn, and visit Bowden, with its charming twelfth-century church, restored earlier this century. The war memorial in this village is actually an adapted sixteenth-century market cross.

You are close to the ruins of the twelfth-century Dryburgh Abbey, founded by the Constable of Scotland, Hugo de Morville, for Premonstratensian monks, and where both Sir Walter Scott and Field-Marshal Haig lie buried. The statue to Sir William Wallace on the river bank was put up by the 12th Earl of Buchan in 1834.

Cross the A699 and go past St Boswell's. This town was a junction for roads from most of the major Border burghs, and the fair on its village green was famous. The Duke of Buccleuch's foxhound kennels are here. This pack, formed by the 5th Duke in 1827, hunts from Hadrian's Wall to Hundy Mundy, and on across Girrick to the Sneep and Mellerstain. Mertoun House, set in the most beautiful 20 acre grounds on the banks of the river Tweed to the east is open to the public. It was designed for the 6th Duke of Sutherland by Sir William Bruce at the beginning of the eighteenth century.

Follow the A68, where you must watch out for fast-moving traffic, and you will be at the beginning of the Dere Street proper. You go through Longnewton Forest, which is only patchy woods these days, and past the site of the Battle of Ancrum Moor, where in 1545 the Earl of Angus and Scott of Buccleuch did some successful English-bashing, killing their opposite numbers Sir Bryan Latoun and Sir Ralph Evers. A ghoulish story about one of the more remarkable Scottish soldiers, the Fair Maid of Lilliard,

tells that she had to fight most of the battle on her stumps after her legs were cut off early on. Beyond is the village of Ancrum itself. Above this village in red sandstone caves overlooking Ale Water are caves where the poet James Thomson once carved his name. This literary shrine is not at all easy to find. You then go under the standing stone on the hill outside Harrietsfield. After the B6400 you will find that crossing the river Teviot means winding off the Roman road to look for the bridge. There is a forestry museum on the Teviot Estate nearby. Teviotdale is the home of the Kerr family, the Marquesses of Lothian. On the other side you cross the A698.

Nearby Jedburgh is a good place to stop for some jethart snails, the local toothcracking toffee. Jedburgh, in the Jed Water valley, is the county town of Roxburghshire, and has always held an important place in the area. It was one of the main border towns, lying directly between Carlisle and Edinburgh, so in the Middle Ages changed hands many times between the Scots and the English invaders.

In 1409 twelfth-century Jedburgh Castle had to be destroyed by the Scots who built it, because it was so often in English hands. It stood derelict for many years before being partly rebuilt to become the town jail in 1825. It is now a reform jail museum. Back in its distant past it had been the place where King Malcolm IV of Scotland died, and where a ghost appeared at King Alexander's wedding to warn of another royal death, his own, which occurred only a little while later in a riding accident.

Jedburgh Abbey was founded in 1118 by the same King David who was responsible for Melrose Abbey, but this time for Augustinian canons from Beauvais. It was pulled down on the orders of the Earl of Surrey in 1523, but in its day it must have been one of the most extraordinary buildings in Scotland. Also in the town is the house where Mary Queen of Scots stayed in 1566. It is a museum now, with souvenirs such as her watch on display. Jedburgh makes a distinction between what are called the Uppies and the Doonies, depending on whether you were born above or below the town's market cross. To celebrate this ancient rivalry the two sides play a kind of handball on Shrove Tuesday.

Like Teviotdale, Ferniehurst Castle to the south is owned by the Kerr family. The first castle was built in the fifteenth century, and the most recent update was by the present Marchioness.

From here to Hindhope the villages and towns disappear, and you enter a wild and unpopulated zone. After Mounthooly, the last farm in the College valley, you pass Baittens, Easter Ulston and Crailinghall to come to Cappuck. There is a Roman fort here, where some sculptures have been found, but little remains now. Rennieston, Harden Mains and Swinside Townfoot bring you to Whitton. The Whitton children's home was built in the fourteenth century as a fortified rectory in the style of those at Corbridge and Elsdon. The list of the parishes surrounding the tiny hamlets goes on. Cunzierton is followed by Philogar, then Upper Chatto, Swinside Townhead and Plenderleigh. After Buchtrig you come to Hindhope on the border, and the end of the Dere Street bridleway. It actually continues into England, over the Pennine Way for Walkers on the Cheviot Hills, down through Otterburn and the MOD Danger Areas, to Corbridge near Hexham in the southern edge of the Northumberland National Park. However Dere Street in England is virtually unrideable due to roads and firing zones.

OS Maps: 73, 74 and 80.

Commercial Riding Centres:
Ferniehurst Mill Lodge, Jedburgh, Roxburghshire TD8 6PQ. Tel: 0835 63279.

Accommodation with stables:
Mr & Mrs R. Dick, Otterburn, Kelso, Roxburghshire. Tel: Morebattle 208. Norman Dalgetty, Jedforest Hotel, Jedburgh, Roxburghshire. Tel: Camptown 274. Mr P. Boyd, Harrietsfield House, Ancrum, by Jedburgh, Roxburghshire. Tel: Ancrum 327. Mrs Ann Fraser, Overwells, Jedburgh, Roxburghshire TD8 6LT. Tel: Jedburgh 63020.

Vet:
Rogerson & Partners, Sydenham Vet Health Centre, Edinburgh Road, Kelso, Roxburghshire TD5 7EV. Tel: 0573 24496.

Farriers:
R. T. Hewit RSS, Heiton, Kelso, Roxburghshire TD5 8LA. Tel: Roxburgh 210. G. J. Johnston RSS, Running Burn, Stichill, Kelso, Roxburghshire TD5 7TE. Tel: 0573 7348.

Further Help:
Mrs Ann Fraser, BHS Access Chairman for Scotland, Overwells, Jedburgh, Roxburghshire TD8 6LT. Tel: Jedburgh 63020.

Hawick Circular Ride

First of all, Hawick is pronounced 'Hoik'. The Hawick Circular Route was set up by a local rider in concert with the Countryside Commission and local farmers. It lies mostly on rights of way, and some permissive paths over the Duke of Buccleuch's estate. The Borders Regional Council publish a leaflet about it which is so simple and useful that it makes you wonder if many other, similar rides might be achieved. And then, if linked to other tracks, there could be the structure for out-and-back rides of 20 to 30 miles in a day, or even long distance post-riding, as it is often termed in Scotland, with overnight stops. However, arranging these overnights for horses and people is one of the most time-consuming parts of organizing a ride, unless routes become established, such as the network of stabling in many of the national parks.

This is simply a 27 mile loop, another weekend ride, around the border town of Hawick in Roxburghshire. Modern Hawick dates from when the English, under the Earl of Sussex, destroyed the place in 1570, and only the Douglas's Black Tower of Drumlanrig survived. For a while that tower belonged to the Buccleuchs, and then it became an inn. William Wordsworth stayed there during his tour of Scotland, and it is now the Tower Hotel. Most of today's buildings date from after the ruinous year of 1570, many during the last 100 years. However, twelfth-century coins have been found in the Mote, a 30 ft high hill, 300 ft round, from which there is a good view of where the Slitrig river meets the Teviot.

Hawick is the biggest of the old Border burghs, built largely on the wool trade. The Wilton Lodge Museum just to the west of the town traces the history of the industry which now sees Hawick woollens sold all over the world. Wilton Lodge, set in a 107 acre park, used to be the home of the Langlands family. Electronics are now a key industry, as are chemicals for the textile plants. For two days every June the town celebrates an event called the Common Riding where the marches of the town, its boundaries, are ridden to commemorate a party of the town's brave lads who routed a band of English raiders at Hornshole in 1514, the year after the massacre of the Scots at Flodden, and captured the Hexham Pennant with the war cry 'Teribus, ye Teriodin!' The Town also put up the Horse Monument, sculpted by W F Beattie in 1914, in the High Street in honour of these chaps.

The A7 north of Hawick is a bad road, but a good place to start the loop. Go towards Muirfield and cross the bridge over Dearly Burn. This will bring you to Clarilaw from where you head off to Appletreehall on a public road. Stay on that public road to Corthill, and then towards Burnfoot. You cross the River Teviot at Haughhead. The Teviot eventually joins the Tweed, the second largest river in Scotland, at Kelso. It has a fair salmon run. However, if the river is in spate go along the busy Denholm road to Haughead from Hawickle. After negotiating the river by whichever way you can, go up the Newcastle road, past the Cauldmill smithy, which will bring you to Cavers church. Opposite this church is a path to the old Cavers church. You go through an iron gate into the park, and then along Cavers Knowes, which is a green track. Follow the Bonchester Bridge road for a third of a mile, and then take the old drove road, which has pretty views. After the abandoned farmhouse of Adderstone Lee head for Coliforthill.

The circular route takes you along the New-castleton road, the Williesthruther road, and the Whitchester road, before you come to the A7 which crosses the Teviot again at Branxholm Bridge. You go right to ford the Borthwick Water at Woodfoot, unless it is in spate when you have to go round to Martin's Bridge and cross it there. Going along the Roberton road and around Borth-augh Hill will bring you to Wilton Burn.

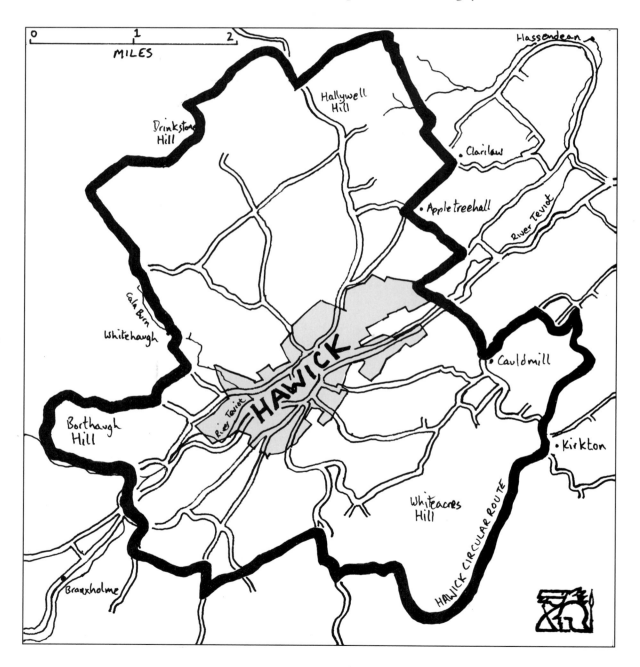

From here there is a public road to Calaburn followed by a drove road to Drinkstone Hill. Go past Long Moss to Groundistone Covert, and then down to Groundistone Moss, which, like Eeyore's Gloomy Place, is rather boggy and sad. Just beyond it is the A7 again.

The long shadows of the north bring out the colours in the border landscape quite startlingly. It is an area steeped in the battles which over the centuries have decided whether it lies in the hands of Edinburgh or London. Almost all the places of interest have some connection with the Border peoples' bloody lives. The walls and four towers of thirteenth-century Hermitage Castle lie about 12 miles south of Hawick. The castle was lived in by the 4th Earl of Bothwell, he who had the love affair with Mary Queen of Scots which involved him murdering her husband Lord Darnley. She later rushed to visit her wounded beau as he lay in the squat fortress, a round trip of 40 miles from Jedburgh. In a colourful history families such as the Dacres, Douglases and Scots of Buccleuch to name but a few have

lived there. It was restored in the nineteenth century. Between here and Hawick are the prehistoric settlements of Dod.

Most of the land you ride through around Hawick belongs to the Duke of Buccleuch. In 1793 the 3rd Duke actually built the village of Newcastleton, to the south on the Liddel Water, specifically for the weaving industry. Another great family from the Hawick area are the Earls of Minto. Minto House, now Craigmount School, which spawned Minto village, six miles north-east of Hawick, was designed for the 1st Earl by Archibald Elliot. Elliot had nothing to do with the rather ugly nineteenth-century church, which was the work of William Playfair. The Elliot family came from Stob's Castle, to the south of Hawick, though they later moved to their Redheugh estate near Newcastleton. Denholm, to the north-east of Hawick, was the birthplace of the poet and orientalist John Leyden in 1776, who was a friend of Sir Walter Scott. There is a memorial obelisk in Denholm to him. The most famous local family were the 'Fighting Turnbulls'. A number of castles and strong-

OS Maps: 79.

Accommodation with stables:
Mr & Mrs Buchanan, Whitfield, Hawick, Roxburghshire. Tel: Hawick 72055. Mrs M. Shiell, Haughhead, Hawick, Roxburghshire. Tel: Hawick 73533. Hazeldean Riding Centre, Hassendeanburn, near Hawick, Roxburghshire. Tel: 0450 87373.

Vets:
Muir Brown & Young MRCVS, Hawick. Tel: Hawick 72038. Gibson & Gibson, Braeside, Gala Terrace, Galashiels, Selkirkshire. Tel: 0896 2156/82716. Rogerson, Baird, Wain & Partners, 120 Galapark, Galashiels, Selkirkshire. Tel: 0896 3759.

Farriers:
E. W. G. Hook DWCF, 7 Union Street, Hawick, Roxburghshire TD9 9LE. J. M. Falla RSS AFCL, Bonchester Bridge, Hawick, Roxburghshire. Tel: Bonchester Bridge 218.

Further Help:
Mrs Ann Fraser, British Horse Society Access Chairman for Scotland, Overwells, Jedburgh, Roxburghshire TD8 6LT. Tel: 0835 63020. Mrs Rathay, Secretary, Hawick Riding Association. Tel: Hawick 75991. Countryside Ranger, Borders Regional Council, Planning Department, Regional Headquarters, Newtown St Boswells. Tel: 0835 23301

A BHS ride around the Hawick Circular. (BHS/Quentin Mclaren.)

The Hawick Circular Ride at Adderstone Lee. (BHS/Quentin Mclaren.)

holds in the Hawick area belonged to them, including Bedrule, and the curiously named Fatlips Castle. The founder of Glasgow University in 1451 was William Turnbull, Bishop of Glasgow.

Bonchester Bridge, to the east of Hawick, which serves the Wauchope Forest, lies on the Rule Water in the dawn shadow of Bonchester Hill. There is an imposing nineteenth-century house here called Greenriver House, and evidence of a prehistoric settlement. To the south is the eighteenth-century St Mary's church. It stands on the site of an earlier church where one day in 1342 Sir William Douglas, of those 'Black Douglases', who lived at Hermitage Castle, burst in and kidnapped the Sherriff of Teviotdale, Warden of the East March, Sir Alexander Ramsay, claiming the Middle March and Ramsay's home Roxburgh Castle as ransom.

The people of the Borders were always known for their cattle rustling. The Armstrongs and Scotts of Buccleuch were infamous *reivers*, the Borders' word, and greatly feared in England. In 1530 James V of Scotland captured Johnny Armstrong by deception and hanged him. A memorial in Teviothead says that Johnny 'rode ever with twenty-four able gentlemen well horsed; yet he never molested any Scottishmen'. The former Scott tower-house Goldielands on the Teviot was where the head of that clan was hanged from his own gateway for snaffling livestock.

The Tower of Branskome was the setting for much of *The Lay of the Last Minstrel* where 'nine-and-twenty nights of fame hung their shields', though judging by its size it must have been a bit cramped. And along with Johnny Armstrong, Henry Scott Riddell lies full five feet under at Teviothead church, who wrote the song *Scotland Yet*.

Wales

The view into the sheltered Usk valley from Allt yr Esgair. (David Ward.)

Glyndŵr's Way

This is a 120-mile route, primarily intended for walkers, running from Offa's Dyke at Knighton, central Powys, westwards to Machynlleth through the mountains, then back east to rejoin the Dyke at Welshpool in north Powys. It might take a week to go its entire length. It is by no means impossible to ride, but it is for the experienced and adventurous rider inclined towards trail-blazing. On the uplands there are areas of bog where the path is ill-defined, and riders need to be able to navigate accurately by compass. It is named after Owain Glyndŵr, the early fifteenth-century Welsh warrior-statesman who devoted his life to fighting the English. He actually came close to forming an independent and united Welsh nation.

The Countryside Commission says that it will be setting up a feasability study into this route as soon as possible with the aim of making it one of the new National Trails. The criteria are that each trail should allow the public to make extensive journeys on foot, horseback or bicycle on routes that, for the most part, do not pass along roads used by motor vehicles. An influx of riders would not be welcome unless there was an established and constantly maintained route. Local farmers give permission for riding through their land if asked, but if not asked take exception.

Starting at Knighton on the Llandridod road, you ride past the Teme Valley Foxhound Kennels. Follow the Wilcome Brook, by Ebrandy House and you come to Craig-y-don Wood, which was named after the Celtic mother goddess Don. Another similar-sounding name connected with the place belonged to Donna, a seventh-century

hermit who lived off roots and berries. Along the farm track the Devil's chair is a famous cleft in the rocks which reputedly leads to an underground passage connecting with Skyborry on the other side of the valley. The spring at the furthest western end of the wood has the distinction of being the site of the murder which lead to the last conviction and hanging in Radnor. The felon, Harley, was suspended by the neck in Presteigne in 1850.

After leaving Knucklas Lane which goes on towards the Old Knighton Racecourse, you follow a ridge to Fountainhead. At Knucklas, there was an Ordovices settlement, a tribe of unusually tall ginger-haired people. It is also the village which Welsh stories record as the venue for the wedding of King Arthur and Guinevere. Apparently the Giants of Bron Wrgan had captured her brothers, so King Arthur went in, Excalibur flailing. He killed them all, and Guinevere's father, another giant called Godfran Gawr, was so grateful that he gave the hero his daughter.

Knucklas Castle was built by Ralph Mortimer in the thirteenth century, but razed to the ground by Owain Glyndŵr in 1402. It was in this state that Edward IV inherited it from his Mortimer born mother. Since then the stones have been thankfully received by the local inhabitants to build their own homes, not to mention the local railway viaduct. After Fountainhead the bridleway goes towards Llancoch, which sits on the railway tunnel outside Llanguallo station, the main Shrewsbury–Swansea line. On the way it passes a barrow called The Camp, where gold coins hidden during the Civil War were found in the nineteenth century. From here onwards the scenery becomes a little wilder; hill farms on open moorland. As the wind bites right through you across this exposed landscape it won't help much to

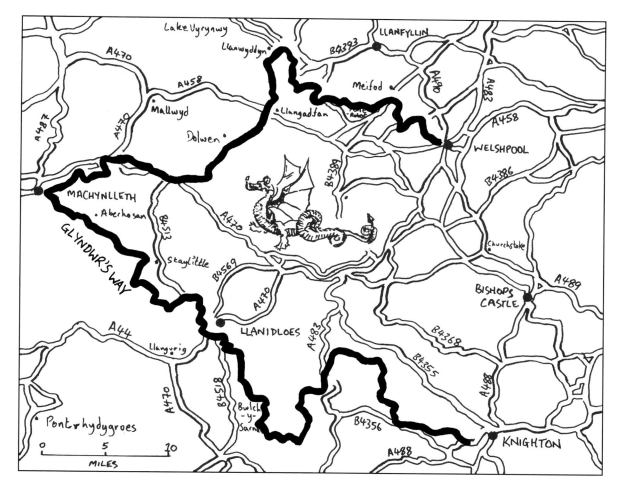

know that Ferley, the next hamlet, comes from the Welsh word for chilly. Beyond it is the rampart at Short Ditch, which was built by Sir Edmund Mortimer at the end of the thirteenth century to halt Owain Glyndŵr's advance from the west. Cross that to come to the derelict Beacon Lodge on Beacon Hill on which there are a number of Bronze Age barrows, and from which there are outstanding views of the Radnor Forest. After Stanky Hill and the Black Mountain you reach Cefn Pawl. From here there are views of the Kerry Mountains beyond the Teme valley.

Beguildy can count two notable necromancers among its former inhabitants. The first was Dr John Dee, the astrologer and mathematician at the court of Elizabeth I who was the model for Prospero in Shakespeare's *The Tempest*. There was also the Beguildy vicar who practised the black arts, and was finally caught trying to fix the result of a local wrestling match with the aid of evil spirits.

Past Wharf Inn, Upper House Farm and Ty'n y bryn is Crug y Byddar. The biggest of the mounds you will see is thought to be the remains of the castle of Uther Pendragon, the father of King Arthur. After Hope's Castle Farm and the Barrows the bridleway goes sharply south towards Penybank. If you haven't been dogged by bad weather you should expect to spend your first night near here.

Llanbadarn Fynydd draws its name from St Padarn, the saint who with St Teilo accompanied Wales's patron, St David, in an effort to break the clergy of Wales away from the clutches of the Archbishop of Canterbury. St Padarn was not always as holy as you would expect. He quarrelled with King Arthur, and struck a hole in the ground at Llanbadarn, burying the unfortunate monarch up to the neck, and kept him there until Arthur came round to the Saint's point of view. Llanbadarn, along with towns all over the west of Britain, has put in a claim for Mons Badonicus, Badon Mount, as the site of King Arthur's last battle. You cross the river Ithon on the way to Moel-dod.

After Ysgwdffordd you follow the Bachell Brook to come to Tyfaenor. From the ridge above the brook there are some beautiful views. Tyfaenor manor house was built by Sir Richard Fowler during the reign of James I of England in the seventeenth century using stone from the demolished Cwmhir Abbey. That the Fowlers were enormously wealthy is remembered in a local ditty:

> Alas! Alas! Poor Radnorshire,
> Never a park, nor ever a deer,
> Nor ever a squire of five hundred a
>   year,
> Save Richard Fowler of Abbey
>   Cwmhir.

The outlines of windows walled up during the 150 dark years of the hated Window Tax are visible. It is now owned by the Griffiths family.

It was Cadwallon ap Madoc who founded the Cistercian Abbey Cwmhir. The building was designed on a magnificent scale and could have been among the five largest in Britain, had it not been destroyed by Owain Glyndŵr in 1401 before its completion. Although the monks struggled to rebuild it they were overtaken by the reformation in 1536. Some of the stonework was saved and taken to Llanidloes church, further along Glyndŵr's Way. After Esgair and the Upper Esgair Hill you pass the barrows at Castell-y-Garu where prehistoric people once buried their dead in stone caskets. At this point Glyndŵr's Way plunges off cold moors into wooded valleys and back again. The area around Bwlch-y-Sarnau is wild territory indeed. It is the parish of St Harmon which comes from St Garmon, St Germanus, who is buried on the Mount, to the west.

Bailey Bog is at the bottom of Bailey Hill, and beyond is Brondrefach. The scenery around here, Waunmarteg, Pistyll, and Prysgduon is craggy, rocky and desolate, though the going along the Way is good. After Blaentrinant the track wiggles through the Rhyd Hywel Hills.

Llanidloes, the next piece of civilization, and probably where you will sleep your second night, was the first town on the river Severn. It was named after St Idloes, and the church of St Idloes overlooks the meeting of the rivers Severn and Clywedog. St Idloes himself was the grandson of a hero named Llawfrodedd Coch, who held the position of one of the three guardians of the cattle of Mudd Hael, a Celtic god.

Leaving the river Clywedog to the west you head out of Llanidloes past Alltgoch. At Y Fan head due west and come down at the foot of the lake Llyn Clywedog. This was opened in 1967, purportedly to stop the lower Severn from flooding. It holds some 11 billion gallons of water, drowning for all time the town of Ystradhynod. The Iron Age fort of Pen-y-Gaer is on its bank. The pile of stones there was left by a giantess who was gathering them in her apron when

A good gallop along the tops over typical Glyndŵr's Way countryside. (Picture courtesy of Tom Linfoot)

the string holding it broke. There are some lovely views of the Severn valley from the hills around the Llyn Clywedog. At the lake head is Staylittle, so called because the farrier here used to reshoe your animal extremely quickly. It was a well-known stopping point for eighteenth-century drovers heading east over the marches with their livestock. The Way goes out through the local Quaker cemetery, which was a popular cause in these parts during the early eighteenth-century, and into the Plynlimon foothills.

After Rhiw-defeitty-fawr farm Glyndŵr's Way crosses a bleak moor. It goes past the small Roman fort at Penycrocbren, overlooking the Afon Clywedog. From Bryn y Fedwen there is a good view of Glaslyn, the lake whose blueness led to the local belief that it was bottomless. Just beyond is the gorge of Foel Fadian through which flows the Afon Dulas. Nant y Fyda is next, and in the valley of the Afon Carog is Aberhosan. This place used to be famous for its wood-carvers, who constructed the fabulously ornamental bardic chairs at the local and national Eisteddfods.

After the bleak exposure of the hill outside Aberhosan, Cefn Modfedd, fir trees mingle with birch, beech and oak around the hamlet of Forge. This brings you to the town of Machynlleth, which marks the turning point of Glyndŵr's Way. From now on the route

veers east as it heads back towards the Marches and England. There is a half timbered eighteenth-century building called the Owain Glyndŵr Institute on the site where that great warrier held his first parliament in 1404. It is now a café, and the home of the Mid Wales Tourist Authority.

After Penegoes, the next village, ride up the steep and sometimes slippery track onto the bracken moorland of Carregyfudde, and then down into the valley in which stands the old textile mill town of Abercegir. Although nothing now remains of the industry which once made the town an important centre in the area, there are still vestiges of its glory in the rows of terraced houses built for the mill workers, and so familiar in valleys of South Wales. Following the farm track along Cefn Côch, the ridge just beyond Abercegir, you will have a beautiful view of Cader Idris in the distance. As the Way comes off the hill towards Cemmaes Road it passes an ancient standing stone. Cemmaes Road is the junction of railways which go to Dolgellau, Newton and back to Machynlleth. Cemmaes itself is connected to the sixth-century St Tydacho who founded the church in the town.

After following the railway you veer to the left to Pen y Gyrn and Commins Gwalia. You have to join a road for a couple of hundred yards, but it is unmetalled. There

OS Maps: 136, 148, 135, 125.

Accommodation with stables:

Mrs F. M. Hrynczak, Y Goedwig, Corris, Macchynlleth, Gwynedd. Tel: Corris 203. Mrs S. Shelswell, Cerniau, Foel, near Welshpool, Powys. Tel: 0743 4721. Mrs M. Payne, Heath Cottage, Forden, near Welshpool, Powys. Tel: Forden 453. Mr R. M. Oliver, Cefn Coch Pony Trekking Centre, Cefnoch, Llanfair Caereinion, Powys, Tel: 0938 810247. Mrs G. Rowlands, Cwmllwydion Farm, Llandinam, Powys SY17 5DJ. Tel: 0686 84314. Mrs C. Davies, The Meadows, Churchstoke, Powys. Tel: Churchstoke 242. Mrs J. Bennett, Trellwydion Farm, Llanbister, Llandridod Wells, Powys LD1 6TH. Tel: Llananno 278.

Vets:

G. M. Jenkins BVSc MRCVS, Craigle, Craig Fach, Machynlleth, Montgomery, Powys. SY20 8BB. Tel: 0654 710416. Thomas Jones & Co., Halfron Surgery, Llanidloes Road, Newtown, Powys SY16 1HA. Tel: 0686 84245.

Farriers:

Stephen Graham Eaton, Aberbechan

Cottage, Aberbechan, near Newtown, Powys SY16 3AS. Tel: Abermule 330. James Patrick Blurton, Rose Mill, Kingswood Lane, Forden, Welshpool, Powys. Tel: Knockin 305. Mark Robert Evans DWCF, Maes y Fynnon, Farrington Lane, Knighton, Powys LD7 1KB. Tel: 0547 528481.

Further Help:

Mrs Daphne Tilley, Blas Isaf, Bryn Rhyd y Arian, Llansannan, near Denbigh, Clwyd LL16 5NR. Tel: 0745 77227. Mrs C. Davies, British Horse Society Powys (North), The Meadows, Churchstoke, Powys. Tel: Churchstoke 242. Jim Saunders, Recreational Paths Officer, Offa's Dyke Centre, West Street, Knighton, Powys. Tel: 0547 528192. Mr P. Wharton, County Architects and Planning Office, Powys County Council, County Hall, Llandridod Wells, Powys LD1 5LE. Tel: 0597 3711. Mrs J. Brown, Secretary Long Distance Riding Group, Vyrnwy Mid Wales, Olympus, Brockhurst Road, Monks Kirby, Rugby, Warwickshire CV23 0RA. Tel: 0788 832581.

are fine views from the gently rolling hills here of the Dyfi Valley. In order to reach Llanbrynmair you go past Brynmoel and Gwern y Bwlch, and follow the fast and furious A470. In Llanbrynmair the Pudding Festival, on St Bartholomew's day, is a pagan festival of charity where farmers give milk to the poor to make puddings with.

For several miles now you ride through a desolate wilderness. It is hard on the hooves and rugged, but fabulous in its solitude. It is dangerous to attempt it in bad weather. The next civilization is Llangadfan. Cwm Carneddl, the valley of the stones, is named after Owain the robber's grave, the barrow you pass. He had been casing a joint in the area when a small army of locals appeared armed with an array of farmyard weaponry. He rode hell for leather from Owen's Ford, chased by the pitchfork-brandishing crew, all the way to Stirrup Bog, where his stirrups broke, and they lynched him.

After Bryn Gwyn and Tyn y gors, you follow the charming Afon Gam, with its tiny tributaries running off the heather-clad hills and small valleys. You go all the way to the conspicuous Fort Moelddolwen, which at 100 yards in length and surrounded by ditches and ramparts must have been an important prehistoric farming community. There are few signposts throughout that section so don't leave the Gam valley until the fort. Llangadfan takes its name from St Cadfan.

You have to ride along the A458 for a short while before forking right to go towards the Dyfnant Forest. There is some pretty farmland above the river Banwy, scattered with stones by two fighting giants. The forest is not so easy, because the Forestry Commission keep putting stiles up. However it is crossed by such a maze of tracks there is always a way through. The Dyfnant is an enormous piece of woodland planted with Grand fir, Lodgepole pine, and Sitka spruce, as well as many other types of conifer, and even a few deciduous trees. Halfway through it is the lead mine of Moel Achles. It ends with the little cluster of houses called Ddôl Cownwy, from which it is a short step to Llanwyddyn and Lake Vyrnwy, where you will stay the fifth night.

The river Vyrnwy used to rise in the valley now occupied by the lake. To create a much-needed reservoir for Liverpool it was a simple job to throw a dam across its narrow foot. It is likely that the valley used to be a lake until soon after the last Ice Age anyway. The foundation stone was laid in 1881 by the 3rd Earl of Powys, and the reservoir was working to capacity a mere eight years later. The curious Vyrnwy Tower houses a nineteenth-century water filtration system, but this can only remove the larger impurities, such as fish.

The stretch from Abertridwr to Gallt yr Ancwr is rather dull riding, but there is some pretty scenery along the Vyrnwy valley. After leaving the B4393 the track takes you down to the village of Llwydiarth. The Vaughn family owned Llwydiarth Hall and estates in the area. The Vaughns have held positions and taken stands of national importance since Sir Gryffud Vaughn helped Owain Glyndŵr in his battles with Henry IV. From here there is another short stretch of B road before you head up onto Fridd Llwydiarth.

After Dolwar Hall you pass Dolwar Fach, the farm where Ann Griffiths (the celebrated Welsh hymn-writer) lived.

The mill just outside the village of Dolanog, Felin Dolanog, is where the famous Welsh flannel was bleached. Despite this early pollution, and the mill owner's relentless netting of the river, there is still a good salmon run, and the great beasts have to leap a weir waterfall at the mill. As you follow the Way downstream the hills on either side close in. To the north is Allt Dolanog, which is crowned by a fort called Llys y Cawr, the giant's hall, and to the south is Pen y Berth. If you have by chance picked up an eye infection from your days spent in the saddle the spring water which runs off Pen y Berth is said to be sure to cure you. Pontrobert was named after its builder in 1670, the philanthropist Oliver ap Robert.

On leaving Meifod you follow the river path from Broniarth Bridge and up through the woods to cross the Broniarth Hills. If you look back from the top you will see some startling views of Meifod and beyond. The Way goes near Cefn Pentre, past an Iron Age fort and the outer defences of Mathrafal Palace. It potters through several woods, including Kennel Wood, hunted by the Tanatside Hounds. You follow Laundry Lane to the crossroads, and the road brings you at last to Welshpool, where Glyndŵr's Way connects with Offa's Dyke, which cannot be ridden in its entirety at this time. Welshpool, named Pool after the de la Pole family who owned the castle, was given its prefix so that it wouldn't be confused with Poole in Dorset.

St Mary's church has part of the roof from the Abbey of Strata Marcella, and the stone near the door was used by the abbot as a throne. The remains of this great Cistercian foundation lie to the east.

Southern Cambrians

The horse is still king in the southern Cambrian Mountains, haunt of the red kite, lying across the border between Powys and Dyfed. Throughout the centuries drovers on horseback have brought their Welsh black cattle across the eastern hills from this wilderness to sell in England. Horses are still used to gather sheep, a marvellous sight, and this was the last bastion of the horse as the main local transport. Some of the hardiest and most courageous animals in Britain are bred here in the greatest Welsh cob studs, which regularly sell their young stock to the continent for record prices.

The area is roughly oblong, bordered by the Brechfa Forest to the south-west, the B4343 to the north-west, Glyndŵr's Way to the north-east and the A483 to the south-east. Although it abounds in bridleways they are either not on the map or shown differently, or else they have been blocked. The riding is superb, but visitors would soon be either hopelessly lost or bogged, unless guided by a local. There are at least ten long distance rides in the southern Cambrians, routes of 20 to 50 miles, but many of them have sections passable with owners' permission only, and it is unlikely that these landowners would welcome casual use, as it would open the path up too much, and possibly precipitate claims for a proper bridleway.

Llanwrtyd Wells was a spa town, and it is easy to see why the Victorians were attracted to it. It has superb views over the hills to the east, the Mynydd Eppynt. It is now an important trekking centre and routes stretch away from it towards the Monks' Trod and the Tyw Forest. Llandovery, down the busy A483 is a pretty market town with a cobbled square, but not such a good centre for riding.

On the line of the Cambrians north-east from the Brechfa Forest you come to Pumsaint, which means Five Saints, and has a stone, marking the spot where a set of quintuplet saints once spent the night. They lend their names to the local church. This Hamlet overlooks the river Cothi. The National Trust owns the Roman gold mines to the east, the Caeo Caves. On the north bank of the river Teifi is Lampeter, whose famous horse fair takes place in May.

The Talbot Hotel in Tregaron is the best place to start a tour of the southern Cambrians. It is famous for the Welsh hospitality and good food, and its bar is crowded with local Welsh characters. It is quite common for the hillfarmers to be running herds of 60 breeding pony mares on their open mountain, and the Talbot is the place to talk to them. Tregaron is a small market town and one of the most important trekking centres in Wales. A mile north of the town is the Bog of Tregaron. Cors Caron, at four miles long the largest in Britain. It is still expanding and is now a nature reserve highly favoured by botanists.

There is a trotting race club in Tregaron and meetings are held throughout the summer. It is an exciting sport and most entertaining to watch. There are also local hunts. They aren't as sophisticated as the best of the English, but they are friendly, and exciting days can be had on the mountain. 20 miles to the north of Tregaron is the famous Devil's Bridge. There are now three bridges over one another crossing this spectacular gorge of the River Mynach. The lowest one, built in the twelfth century, is the actual Devil's Bridge. The Mynach meets the Rheidol at this point and the two join with a series of

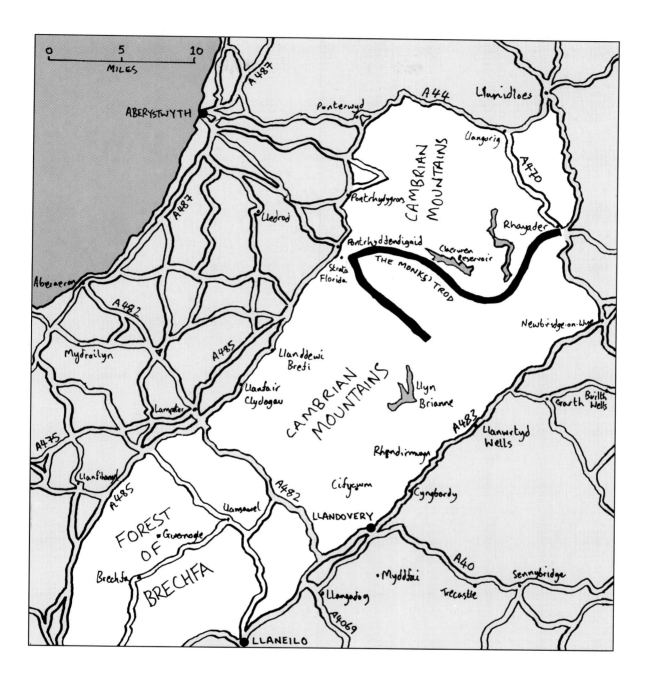

Abergorlech in the Brechfa Forest. (Picture courtesy of Blue Well Riding Centre)

cascading waterfalls.

The Monks' Trod is a bridleway which crosses the Cambrians. It was originally a route between the Abbey Cwmhir on Glyndŵr's Way and Strata Florida Abbey. There are also bridleways north and east to Newtown and Shropshire from Abbey Cwmhir, and several through the woodland of Creigiau. The first part of the Monks' Trod follows the road to Rhayader. This quiet market town marks the convergence of a number of roads. After Rhayader follow the beautiful river Wye downstream before cutting east over the Afon Elan and towards Elan Village. The most exciting part is from here onwards, along the line of the reservoirs Caban-coch and Claerwen.

The Elan Valley reservoirs were begun in 1892, and the last one was opened by the Queen in 1952. They supply water to the Midlands, sixty million gallons a day to Birmingham alone, and the Claerwen Reservoir, which holds ten billion gallons, has at 184 ft the highest gravity dam in the country, across which the bridleway passes. Among the houses these great lakes drowned was one lived in by the poet Shelley. The route goes on over the Cambrian ridge and along the valley of the Mwyro. However, Dyfed County Council say that is has no official status and indeed is not registered as a public right of way within Dyfed.

Due to a four wheel drive vehicle rally in the autumn of 1988 the whole of the Monks' Trod became nearly impassable, even to the native shepherding ponies. However, there are plenty of other places to ride in the area. There are vast tracts of Forestry Commission land and open mountain, although much of these require permission. Similarly there are drovers' roads, including one which goes from Abergavenny to Hay-on-Wye, but

OS Maps: 136, 146 & 147.

Commercial Trekking Centres:
Mr H. Davies, Overland Pony Trek, Dyffryn Farm & Trekking Centre, Rhayader Road, Llanwrthwl, Llandridod Wells, Powys. Tel: 0597 810402. A. & D. Garaway, Trefenter Trekking Centre, Lluest, Trefenter, Aberystwyth, Dyfed SY23 4HG. Tel: 0974 6264. Avril Henn, Bryn Llin Riding Holiday Centre, Bwlchllan, near Lampeter, Dyfed SA48 8QR. Tel: 0974 23351. John Jones, Tregaron Pony Trekking Association, Tregaron, Dyfed. Tel: 0974 294364. The Welsh Long Distance Riding Centre, Pine Lodge Stables, Rhydargaeau, near Carmarthen, Dyfed SA32 7JL. Tel: 0267 253250. Major and Mrs J. B. Gibbins, Blue Well Riding Centre, Ffynnonias, Llanllwni, Dyfed SA39 9AY. Tel: 0267 202274. Mr & Mrs C. Pollak, Cae Iago Trekking Centre, Farmers, Llanwrda, Dyfed SA19 8LZ. Tel: Pumsaint 303. Lluest Riding and Trekking Centre, Beili Bedw, Llandeusant, near Llangadog, Dyfed. Tel: 0550 4661. Mrs D. Whiting, LDL Trekking Centre, Pant-y-Rhedyn, Llandysul, Dyfed SA44 4ET. Tel: Pencader 244.

Accommodation with stables:
Mrs J. Bennet, Trellwydion Farm, Llanbister, Llandridod Wells, Powys LD1 6TH. Tel: Llananno 278. Mrs Carpenter, Pen-y-Craig Farm, Llandeilo Graban, Erwood, Builth Wells, Powys. Mrs P. Conn, Penpompren, Tregaron, Dyfed. Mrs Davies, Moelfryn Mawr, Bethania, Dyfed. Mrs S. Johnson, Rhiwlas Isaf, Cilcennin, Tregaron, Dyfed. Mrs A. Kibble, Tynrhos, Newbridge-on-Wye, Llandridod Wells, Powys. Tel: Newbridge-on-Wye 425. Mrs G. Rowlands, Cwmllwydion Farm,

Llandinam, Powys SY17 5DJ. Tel: 0686 84314. The Talbot Hotel, Tregaron, Dyfed. Mrs B. Williams, Dol-Llyn-Wydd Farm, Builth Wells, Powys LD2 3RZ. Tel: 0982 553660. Mrs E. Davies, Ffos-yffin Fawr, Capel Den, Carmarthen, Dyfed SA32 8AG. Mrs C. R. James, Tyllwyd Hir, Llanwrda, Dyfed SA19 8AS. Tel: Llangadog 777307.

Vets:
T. G. G. Herbert, Manor Hall, Lampeter Road, Aberaeron, Dyfed SA46 0ED Tel: 0545 570690. Thomas Jones & Co, Hafron Surgery, Llanidloes Road, Newtown, Powys SY16 9HA. Tel: 0686 84245. Tysul Veterinary Group, Pencader Road, Llandyssul, Dyfed. Tel: 0559 323318.

Farriers:
T. F. J. Benson RSS, Fynnon-Newydd, Cross Inn, Llanon, Dyfed. Tel: Nebo 309. V. C. M. Davies RSS, The Smithy, Abermagwr, Aberystwyth, Dyfed SA14 7DF. Tel: Crosswood 296. D. Morgan RSS Hons & E. L. Morgan DWCF, Plasnewydd, Farmers, Llanwrda, Dyfed, SA19 8JF. Tel: 0558 5267. P. A. Rail RSS, Maespwll, Talgarreg, Llandysul, Dyfed. Tel: Pontshean 385.

Further Help:
Sally Roberts, Chairman Vale of Aeron Riding Club and British Horse Society Long Distance Ride Organizer, The Annexe, Navy Hall, Bronnaut, Aberystwyth, Dyfed. Tel: 0974 21634. Mrs E. Bignell, British Horse Society, 18 Hollcombe Avenue, Llandridod Wells, Powys. Tel: 0597 3692. D. W. Henman, Brechfa Forest Manager, Forestry Commission District Office, Maesygroes, Brechfa, Carmarthen, Dyfed SA32 7RB. Tel: 0267 89244.

they are a long way from being formalized, waymarked or regularly used at all, except by the natives.

To the south west is the Brechfa Forest. This mature Forestry Commission plantation lies just on the edge of the Brecon Beacons. The rides here are centred on Rhydcymerau and Gwernogle. Brechfa itself, nine miles north-east of Carmarthen, sits quietly in the bowl of the Cothi valley. Its bijou quality is enhanced by the creeper-covered Forester's Arms inn, squat rectory, and a house dating from the middle ages with its own chapel. Even the council houses are unobtrusive. Nantyaredig in the Towy valley is south of Brechfa, and beyond it there is a group of standing stones.

Following the Cothi east you come to Abergorlech, which is eight miles north of Llandeilo. The brightly polished oil lamps at the restored church have always been worth visiting. The village also has a fine three-arched bridge. Up through the trees and Gavernoghe to the north is the open mountain overlooking Llanbydder in the Teifi valley. This little market town is four miles south of Lampeter, centred around the church by the river. The church has been largely restored, and the tower is extremely fine. Above it the pointed arch windows of the Cross Hands Inn stare down on the market cross. The town's horse fair is famous throughout South Wales. The Mart takes place on the last Thursday of every month. The best deals on the ponies and hunters available can be made at the public bar of the Black Lion. Perhaps you could start your tour of the Brechfa bridleways by buying yourself a solid and reliable cob!

Between Llanbydder and Llandysul on a bridge there is an incongruous cross informing the world that in 1822 the county planning office, in typical style, agreed with the bridge-users that the bridge was really a bridge. The moor further south, beyond the tumuli at Pen-gaer, is Mynydd Llanybyddar, which is over 1,300 ft in places, marking the border of the Brechfa Forest.

Through a short gorge, the road to the west brings you over to the top of the Afon Gwili. Further on it comes to Llanllawddog, with its unaffected nineteenth-century church.

Brecon Beacons

This 520 square mile wilderness, mostly in Powys, of mountains, forests, caves, waterfalls and valleys, runs from the Black Mountain to the west, through the Fforest Fawr and the Brecon Beacons themselves, to the Black Mountains in the east. Only 35,000 people live there. Some centres operate trail riding over a wide area, with overnight stops, especially from the east end of the park. They tend to use the indigenous Welsh ponies and cobs, between 12 and 15 hands. If you set out on your own, note that common land is not necessarily open access just because it is unenclosed. Anyone organizing a ride in the area should obtain the consent of landowners. There is no useful continuous route across the park from east to west, but there are a number of bridleways. There used to be a Black Mountain Ride, but it is

no longer held as it is considered that the course is too dangerous. Dangerous or challenging landscape is, of course, a feature of the national parks, and the increase in riding might mean that the authorities will establish set routes in the area.

Llandeilo, a small market town in the Towy valley, is a good starting point. Above it, on stone rich with fossils, is the castle of Dinefwr, where Lord Rhys once lived, as well as Sir Richard ap Thomas, chief of the Tudors. After Llandyfan, once a centre for smelting iron, you come to twelfth-century Carreg Cennen Castle, three miles southeast of Llandeilo. This was also built by Lord Rhys, and although not so hot architecturally, it was situated magnificently on towering limestone cliffs. The corner towers and gateway are all that remain of the vandalism of 500 Yorkists who smashed the place to pieces with 'bar, picks and crowbars of iron'. Bethlehem, further on, is named after its nonconformist chapel, like many

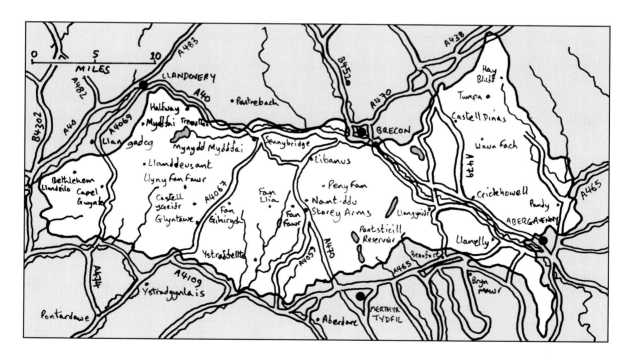

A ridge called Cat's Back in the Black Mountains. (Picture courtesy of Mills Bros.)

hamlets in Wales. To the east there are the remains of a Roman villa, and at Garn Goch a hillfort built in the Iron Age, the civilization the Romans succeeded.

Y Mynydd Du, the Black Mountain, is the beginning of a superb weatherbeaten escarpment which goes as far as Hay, along the Wye valley, where it stands 2,000 ft high. Brecknock Fan is the highest point of the Black Mountain, commanding views over the Bristol Channel to Exmoor in the south, and to Cader Idris in the north. While riding around here you might put up the odd brown hare.

Pontarllechau is a centre for the quarrying of tilestones. In the Llanddeusant area there are a lot of bronze age burial mounds. However, for real wizardry go to Myddfai. A farmer there once married a fairy from the magic lake of Llyn-y-Fan Fach. She ran away after he had hit her three times with an object containing iron, and returned to her lake never to be seen again. Her magic however continued in her descendants, who were known as the Physicians of Myddfai. The last one died earlier this century.

The river Usk flows out of the Usk Reservoir. It is the largest river in the park, rises in the western moors and leaves the park near Abergavenny. It is fed on the way by streams coming off the sandstone of the uplands, through gorges in the limestone, quite unlike any other river in Wales, and it provides a habitat for the otter, dipper, pied wagtail, kingfisher, sandpiper, and brown trout. It has a good salmon run as well. Another interesting animal lives at Lywel. The vicar there really does have bats in his belfry. A colony of rare natterer bats live in the fifteenth-century tower of the church,

The Black Mountains above Talgarth. (Picture courtesy of Mills Bros.)

which also contains stones carved with sixth- and seventh-century inscriptions.

Up the road are the Bronze Age circles of the imponderable Trecastle Mountain. The mound with the spinney of beech trees in Trecastle itself is the site of one of the largest castles in the park, originally built as an outpost by the Lord of Brecon in the twelfth century. Further along the Usk valley, Sennybridge is dominated by the army camp which trains on the ranges of Mynydd Epynt. It lies on the River Senni opposite the Castell Du where poachers were imprisoned by the Constable of the Fforest Fawr in the fourteenth century. The larch copses at Penpont were put in as part of the landscaping of the Williams' house in the eighteenth cen-

tury. A more deadly species of tree lurks at fourteenth-century St Catwg's church at Llanspiddid. For goodness sake don't tether your horse to the churchyard's famous yews.

Brecon, where the Honddu meets the Usk, has been an important city since William the Conqueror arrived. It was the Norman William de Braose who succeeded to the Neufmarchés and incited the Brecon citizens to lynch the young Trahairn of Wales. His family cropped up later in the earlier chapter on the Downs Link Path in connection with more castles. It was the Normans who built this castle, which was finally destroyed by the townspeople themselves during the civil war to prevent Brecon from becoming simply

The view from Pain's Castle. (Picture courtesy of Mills Bros)

a pawn to be traded: an early example of unilateral disarmament.

Gaer, a couple of miles to the west of Brecon, was the local Roman garrison fort. It was excavated by Sir Mortimer Wheeler in 1925, and he discovered evidence that the Roman legion there had been Spanish cavalry. It is on the crossroads of the road which they built from Abergavenny to Llandovery along the Usk valley and past Y Pigwn, and the north-south road which certainly went through the Ffawr Forest, and probably as far as Llandridod. Just over the River Ysgir is a hump, which is all that remains of a twelfth-century castle, and there is a hill fort to the north-east at Pen-y-Crug.

Moving south-west you come to Llanfrynach, which was named after St Brynach, who was a missionary from Ireland during the fifth century. After it is Llanhamlach, where at Ty Illtyd you will find the best preserved stone dolmens in the park, commemorating the death of a Stone Age man. At Llansantfread the poet Henry Vaughan, who died in 1695, is buried where the new nineteenth-century church St Bride's now stands. There are the embankments of a castle at Blaenllynfi, between Bwlch and Llangorse, which once overlooked the approaches to the eastern edge of the Lordship of Brecknock. In 1522 Leland called it a 'very fair castle, now decaying'. Llangynidr has a curious multi-arched bridge over the Usk, like the one at Crickhowell. At Tretower there is a Norman castle, abandoned in the fifteenth century for a fortified house. It was a farmhouse for a while, but is now looked after by the Department of the Environment.

The Black Mountains lie within the borders set by the Usk, Llynfi and Wye valleys. The peaks of mountains such as Pen Cerrig-Calch at 2,302 ft are too high to ride, but the scenery is magnificent. This is also the nearest range of mountains to London. Crickhowell has a startling view to the south-west of the vast screes of Mynydd Llangatwg. The remains of Crickhowell's medieval castle are interesting, though only one tower and a few smashed walls remain. At Porth Mawr to the west there is the gate of a house built for the Herbert family during the sixteenth century. Sir George Everest lived to the north-west of the town at Gwernvale. In St Catwg's church in Llangattock there are stocks and a whipping post. Past Llangenny is Llanelli, an old iron smelting hamlet. The Clydach gorge comes to the wider Usk valley at Gilwern.

A medieval motte and bailey castle lies in ruins in a park to the south of Abergavenny. Over the mountains of Sugar Loaf and Skirrid Fawr, which have both been cut off from the rest of the Black Mountains by millenia of erosion, you come to Llanfihangel Crucorney, with Llanfihangel Court, a superb gabled house dating from the sixteenth century. Beyond, at Dial Garreg, Richard de Clare was killed by Welsh guerillas in 1135.

Llanthony in the Vale of Eywas is one of the most beautiful parts of this end of the national park. Try to see the stunning ruins of the twelfth-century Llanthony Priory. William de Lacy, the brother of the Lord of Eywas, founded it in the early twelfth century. The Spanish chestnuts were an addition to the nineteenth century by Walter Savage Landor, who decided that he didn't like the place much. Part of it has now been turned into a hotel. The peaks of Hay Bluff, 2,219 ft, and Tumpa, 2,263 ft, separate Llanthony and the Golden Valley from Talgarth, which was important both for its eight annual cattle fairs, and the commanding position it held on the east-west road.

The eighteenth-century Methodist

Llangynidr Bridge, built in about 1600, over the river Usk.

View of Pen-y-fan from Craig Cerrig-gleisiad.

preacher Howell Harris, with the support of the Countess of Huntingdon, founded a self-sufficient community at Trefecca. It was only successful during his lifetime, though. The mountains here are a sandstone called brownstone. The highest, like Pen-y-Gadair Fawr, at 2,624 ft, and Waun Fach, at 2,660 ft, are capped with different conglomerates called the Plateau Beds. Castell Dinas, at 1,476 ft, was called an ancient seat of 'unsociable and distrustfull barons' by Malkin. Although its eleventh-century magnificence has crumbled to the scattered stones from which it was made, it has superb views. It sits on a lonely knob, and around it are Iron Age earthen ramparts. Norman castles were often built in places vacated by prehistoric man.

Llangorse Lake is a natural body of water. However, agricultural effluents have been poured in killing everything in their path. It is a reed-encircled pretty lake, but quite dead. The figure of eight this chapter is describing takes you through Llansantfread and Talybont again, and towards the peaks of the Brecon Beacons, which are assembled in serried ranks over the Usk valley. Pen-y-Fan, 2,906 ft, and Corn Du, 2,863 ft, are the two crowns on a magnificent four mile ridge, a sheer scarp to the north and rolling moorland sloping away to the south, strapped by the pass at Storey Arms. Below Corn Du is the fairy lake fed by the Cwm-llch stream, still haunted by King Arthur. Pontsticill Reservoir, to the south, is the lowest of the reservoirs, opened in 1927. At its foot is Pant, with its narrow guage railway. You are close to the mining valleys such as the Rhondda here. Merthyr Tydfil is just down the Taff Vale.

OS Maps: 146, 159, 160, 161.

Commercial Riding Centres:
Michael and Maria Turner, Trans-Wales Rides, Cwmfforest Riding Centre, Talgarth, Powys LD3 0EU. Tel: 0874 711398. Pegasus Trekking Centre, Goed Farm Partrishow, Abergavenny, Gwent. Tel: 0873 890425. Pengelli Fach Farm, Ponsticill, Merthyr Tydfil, Mid Glamorgan. Tel: Merthyr Tydfil 722169. Tregoyd Pony Trekking Centre, Cadarn Trail Riding Farm, Felindre, Brecon, Powys. Tel: 0497 4680. Mills Bros, Newcourt, Felindre, Three Cocks, Brecon LD3 0SS. Tel: 0497 4285. G. J. Price, Pentwyn, Pengenfford, Talgarth, Brecon, Powys. Tel: Talgarth 711468. A. C. Bentley, Lower Panteg, Pengenffordd, Talgarth, Brecon, Powys. Pinegrove Farm, Llanwenarth Citra, Abergavenny, Gwent. Tel: Crickhowell 810228. T. Powell, Trevelog, Llanthony, Abergavenny, Gwent. Tel: Crucorney 890216. Llan-Gors Trekking and Riding Centre, Pen-y-Bryn, Llan-Gors, Brecon, Powys. Tel: 0874 84272. Ellesmere, Llan-Gors, Brecon, Powys. Tel: Llangorse 252. Llangenny Trekking Centre, Llangenny, Crickhowell, Powys NP8 1HD. Tel: 0873 810175. Wern Riding Centre, Wern Watkin Farm, Llangattock, Crickhowell, Powys. Tel: 0873 810899. Crickhowell Riding Stables, Llangattock, Crickhowell, Powys, Tel: 0873 810244. Upper Cantref Pony Trekking Centre, Llanfrynach, Brecon, Powys. Tel: 0874 86223. Glynhir Lodge Stables, Llandybie, Ammanford, Dyfed. Tel: Llandybie 850664.

Trewsygoed Stud, Fforest, Abergavenny, Gwent. Tel: Crucorney 890296. Neuadd Trekking Centre, Cwmyoy, Abvergavenny, Gwent NP7 7NS. Tel: Crucorney 890276. Grange Pony Trekking Centre, Capel-y-Ffin, Abergavenny, Gwent. Tel: Crucorney 890215. Dan-yr-Ogof Caves, Residential Trekking Centre, Aber-Craf, Swansea Valley, Powys. Tel: Abercrave 730284.

Accommodation with stables:
Wynne Bowen, Upper Pencomyn Farm, Forge Lane, Llangynidr, Crickhowell, Powys NP8 1LU. Tel: 0874 730666. Ty Neuadd International Centre, Neuadd Reservoirs, Torpantau, Merthyr Tydfil, Mid Glamorgan CF48 2UT. Tel: 0685 71889.

Vets:
Abbey Veterinary Centre, Brecon House, Elvicta Estate, Crickhowell, Powys, Tel: Crickhowell 810425. Thomas & Percy, 6 King Street, Llandeilo, Dyfed SA19 6BA. Tel: 0558 282337.

Farriers:
Evan John Lloyd DWCF, Llanfellte Farm, Bwlch, Brecon, Powys LD3 7JL. Tel: 0874 730242. Leonard John Williams RSS, 12 Brynawelon, Trecastle, Brecon, Powys LD3 8UG. Tel: 0874 82237.

Further Help:
Roger Stevens, Information Officer, Brecon Beacons National Park, 7 Glamorgan Street, Brecon, Powys LD3 7DP. Tel: 0874 4437. Michael Turner, British Horse Society, Cwmfforest Riding Centre, Talgarth, Powys LD3 0EU. Tel: 0874 711398.

Vaynor has a thirteenth century church extensively rebuilt in the nineteenth century by a Merthyr Tydfil Ironmaster, Robert Crawshay, who is buried there. On the other side of the valley is Morlais castle. The gorges and waterfalls around Ystradfellte are shaded by ash and carpeted in delicate ferns, and cut by the streams the Nedd, the Mellte, the Hepste and the Pyrddin.

The 40,000 acres of the Fforest Fawr, which begins with Fan Fawr, 2,409 ft, consist of tall rounded hills. It is much less wooded than it was when named in the fourteenth century, but in those days the word forest simply meant hunting ground, and for the King's chase it was, or at least to fill the royal table. Following the line from Fan Llia to Fan Nedd to Fan Gihirych brings you to Fan Hir, whose scarp gradually grows to plummet from the grim purple cliffs over Llyn-y-Fan Fawr, the corrie lake. Maen Mawr is a standing stone, part of a larger circle, to the north of Fan Hir, and to the west is Brecknock Fan at 2,632 ft. Past Glyntawe are the Dan-yr-Ogof Caves, which are well-lit and well visited, but still retain some of their timeless mystique. There were seven medieval mills in the Fforest Fawr, and Dan-yr-Ogof was probably one of them.

This chapter ends with one of the Brecon Beacons more extraordinary characters, Craig-y-Nos was where Madame Adelina Patti lived. She bought it in 1878 and moved in with the tenor Nicolini, whom she married in Ystradgynlais church. He died in 1899 and she married Baron Cederström, from Sweden. She died in her beloved Italianate house in 1919 at the age of seventy-six. It is now a hospital, but the theatre she built for it is still there. Just to the east is the 1,000 acre nature reserve of Ogof Ffynnon Ddu. The heather-covered ground here is home to the ring ouzel, and the calls of the red grouse 'go-back! go-back!' can be heard.

Proposed Bridleways

Crossing the river Gwynfai on the Pilgrim's Ride in the shadow of Snowdon itself. (Picture courtesy of Snowdonia Riding Stables)

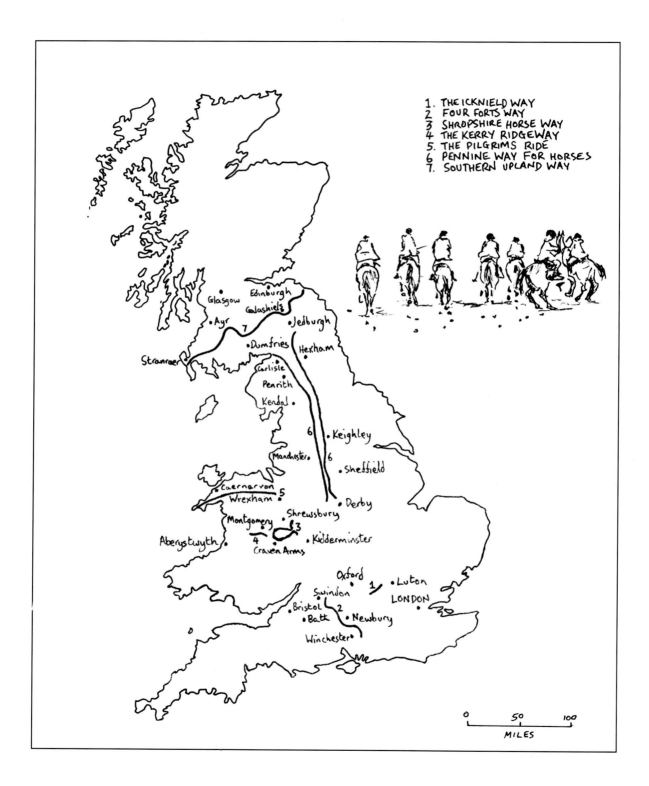

1. THE ICKNIELD WAY
2. FOUR FORTS WAY
3. SHROPSHIRE HORSE WAY
4. THE KERRY RIDGEWAY
5. THE PILGRIMS RIDE
6. PENNINE WAY FOR HORSES
7. SOUTHERN UPLAND WAY

The Icknield Way

This is where the Icknield Way leaves the Swan's Way to go east from Princes Risborough to Ivinghoe Beacon, instead of north. It is not officially waymarked, but has been ridden. It is twelve miles long, less than a day's ride.

From Princes Risborough you go to White-leaf Cross, and then past Chequers mentioned in the chapter on the Swan's Way. On the top of Coombe Hill there is a monument to the men of Buckinghamshire who died in the Boer War. The view northwards from here over the Vale of Aylesbury is magnificent. Wendover is the next town, which, despite the main roads, has kept much of its old charm with its timbered fronts. Cromwell slept in the Red Lion in 1642, and his room is more or less as it was then. After Wendover Woods, the A4011 and the A41 you come to Tring Hill.

Tring is a small town, but noted for its Natural History Museum, which became part of the Natural History collection at South Kensington when Lionel, Lord Rothschild, left his enormous insect collection to the nation. St Peter & St Paul's Church in the town has thirteenth-century parts, and a large fourteenth-century tower. Tring Park was once one of the six great mansions in the area belonging to the Rothschild family, and is now a school. The four Tring Reservoirs are all part of a National Nature Reserve and an important bird sanctuary. The waters feed the Grand Union Canal, near Aldbury, which still has its stocks and whipping post around its village green.

The six square miles of the Ashridge Estate, which now belongs to the National Trust, stretches from here to Ivinghoe Beacon in the north. Halfway across Aldbury Common is a monument to the 3rd Duke of Bridgewater, who died in 1803, and who was the inspiration behind the English canal system. If you climb the 172 steps to the top you will be rewarded by an excellent view.

After Aldbury Nowers you pass an ancient Windmill in a field, which will bring you to Ivinghoe. The King's Head has fifteenth-century origins, and parts of the Church of St Mary the Virgin are thirteenth century, like the twisted faces carved into the poppy heads on the ends of the pews. 756 ft Ivinghoe Beacon was established during Elizabeth I's reign. A pan was kept topped up with pitch in case it had to be lit to call men to arms against a Spanish invasion. From its summit can be seen the Dunstable Downs, the Quainton Hills and most of the Icknield Way along the rest of the Chilterns.

OS Map: 166

Horse-box Parking:
Beacon Hill, near Ivinghoe on the B489.

Vet:
Parker Godsal & Snookes, Vale Cottage, 15 Aylesbury Road, Wendover, Buckinghamshire HP22 6JG. Tel: 0296 623439.

Farrier:
Graham Peter Finnis, 23 Wenwell Close, Aston Clinton, Aylesbury, Buckinghamshire. Tel: Aylesbury 630372.

Further Help:
Mrs Penelope Reid, British Horse Society Bridleways Officer, Morewood House, Hampstead Marshall, Newbury, Berkshire RG15 0JD. Tel: 0488 58823 (or 071 748 9478).

Four Forts Way

This is a proposal made to the Hampshire, Wiltshire and Berkshire County Councils by Brenda Wickham, BHS Bridleways Officer for Buckinghamshire. The route starts at St Catherine's Fort in Winchester, goes north to Arlesford and past Basingstoke. From there it takes in Watership Down, Froxfield, and Ogbourne St George to meet the Ridgeway. It traces the route of a series of early English Hill Forts.

A letter from the Hampshire Recreation Department said, 'Much of the proposed way is on existing bridleways and RUPPs but it is not waymarked and I do not envisage it being given high priority in the foreseeable future.' Riders, of course, will always use 'existing bridleways and RUPPs', and create their own rides within that network, long distance or otherwise. The obvious desired trend would be the creation of named, official routes, with shorter loops off a waymarked backbone, supported by special guides and maps.

OS Maps: 174, 175, 185.

Further Help:
Mrs Brenda Wickham, British Horse Society County Bridleways Officer, Chiltern Lodge, Upway, Chalfont St Peter, Buckinghamshire SL9 0AS. Tel: 0753 882827.

Denizens of the New Forest.

Shropshire Horse Way

This is otherwise known as the Princess Royal Route, because of her future involvement in the ride's feature of providing special areas for disabled riders.

It is a large, roughly circular route in central Shropshire, but although it is not yet established or waymarked, a feasability study has been published of considerable detail. The route is to be tied in with other leisure activity areas such as the new Severn Valley Park, Ironbridge with its industrial history museums and the Telford Town Centre Park. The western end of the route, encompasses Long Mynd with its earth barrows, the eastern end Much Wenlock, Telford to the north, and a spur to Highley Country Park in the south.

The British Horse Society Bridleways Officer for Shropshire, Donald Pearse, has worked out an extensive account of this proposed route, based on his 25 years' experience of riding on the Marches. Broadly, he proposed to the Council two or more parallel tracks close enough for riders to make their way from one to the other.

OS Maps: 126, 127, 137 and 138.

Further Help:
Donald Pearse, British Horse Society Bridleways Officer for Shropshire, Woodley, Burway Road, Church Stretton, Shropshire SY6 6DP. Rights of Way Department, Shropshire County Council, Shrewsbury SY2 6ND.

Galloping close to the northern branch of the Shropshire Horse Way. The southern route goes along the top of the Long Mynd on the skyline. (Picture courtesy of Tom Linfoot)

Kerry Ridgeway

The Kerry Ridgeway, which has already been ridden, will become part of a link between the Shropshire Horse Way and a trans Wales route, along the portions of Glyndŵr's Way. It crosses the tops of the Kerry Hills from Cider House Farm to Bishops Castle along the partly forested hard-won border between Shropshire and Powys. It is quite an easy ride, for there are no steep climbs along the ridge, but rather dull.

It crosses a number of dykes and ditches, including Offa's Dyke. Some could have been the boundaries of prehistoric communities, or perhaps early tollbooths. There are a number of barrows along the path, known locally as tumps. The Caer Din Ring is the remains of an Iron Age hillfort, but the motte and bailey Bishopsmoat Castle is Shropshire's highest fortification, standing 1,000 ft above sea-level. It used to be called Castle Wright, which probably stemmed from Castell Rhudd, the red castle, Llewellyn the Great captured a Castell Hithoet in the thirteenth century, since lost in the mists of history, but at the time it was referred to as Castell Coch, also red castle.

OS Maps: 136, 137.

Vet:
Terry Boundy, Kilaganoon, Montgomery, Powys SY15 6HW. Tel: 0686 81505.

Farrier:
Edward Glyn Jones RSS, Penybont, Carno, Newtown, Powys. Tel: 0686 420224.

Snowdon provides the atmospheric backdrop for this group on the Pilgrim's Ride.
(Picture courtesy of Snowdonia Riding Stables)

The Pilgrims' Ride

This 160 mile ride from Llanfynedd (near Wrexham) goes through some of the most spectacular countryside on North Wales. It finishes at Aberdaron on the Gwynedd coast where the pilgrims of yesteryear crossed the sound to Bardsey Island. Proposed by the North East Wales Committee of the British Horse Society, this route is supported in principle by the Clwyd and Gwynedd County Councils, though the BHS feel they are fighting a rearguard action for better routes and access through Gwynedd. The Countryside Commission is treating it as a proposed regional route, which is more than a local walk or ride while being less than a National Trail in the new Commission terminology. A regional route offers walking, riding or cycling routes of more than a day's duration, is linked to other walks and local walks and rides, and National Trails where these exist, and is planned with accommodation as well as public transport in mind. It also has a name and a logo.

The 20 miles from Llanfynedd to Bodfari has been ridden in the course of a charity ride held in 1988 and is straightforward enough. It starts by going through lead and lime quarries along an old packhorse route for transporting the lead to Liverpool and Lancashire. However, from Bodfari onwards some difficulties are likely to be encountered and some parts of the route are suitable only for the more experienced. Mrs Tilley, mentioned in the fact box, who has ridden the whole way, is prepared to mark the maps of intending riders and to offer more comprehensive advice on stabling and accommodation.

The route from Bodfari goes northwards until turning west a mile or two north of Sodom (yes, Sodom), where it crosses Offa's Dyke. A good, mainly grass track leads to just beyond Trefnant where the Pilgrims' Ride runs along the southern bank of the Elwy for two miles or so. Cefn Caves, on the other side of the river, are notable for their prehistoric remains of men and animals. They are thought to be as much as 50,000 years old.

From Cefn Berain the route traverses and climbs Moel Fodiar, the Afon Aled being crossed at Bryn-y-Rhyd-yr-Arian, close to the ancient palace of Plas Isaf, the home of Mrs Tilley and an obvious information point. Riders should have no problem reaching Plas Isaf.

Thereafter the route crosses some high moorland, skirting Moel Emwnt and dropping into the valley path beside Hendre-ddu. There is a good grass verge alongside the lane from here to Ffridd Ucha, the lane continuing to Plas Maenan on the east bank of the Conwy. There are good facilities here at the Maenan Abbey Hotel, but advice should be sought about the crossing of the river over the small bridge to reach Dolgarrog.

The next leg of this fascinating ride goes over the desolate grandeur of the Snowdonian foothills. Striking north to Tal-y-bont and thence to Hafoty Gwyn and Cae Coch the way follows a small by-road until it hits the Roman road cutting through the pass dividing Tal-y-fan and The Drum and dropping steeply to Aber and the coast. You then go almost due south to Llyn Padarn and Llanberis and thence by a rough, high moorland track to Rhydd ddu and from there along the Dwyfor to Cwm Pennant, one of the most beautiful stretches of the ride but, at the time of writing, not without one or two problems. Advice needs to be sought about the best way to tackle this part of the route which continues over a drove road to Garn Dolbenmaen and Bryncir and to the wild

Moel Smytho near Waun Fawr, with Snowdon in the background. (Picture courtesy of Snowdonia Riding Stables)

wonder of the Lleyn, dominated by the triple peaks of Yr Eifl, called The Rivals by the English, but meaning The Forks in Welsh. Everywhere from here to the tip of the Lleyn at Aberdaron are ancient tumuli and continual reminders of Gallic and Celtic saints, for this is the way of the pilgrim to Bardsey's holy isle. The way is to Llanaelhaearn at the foot of Yr Eifl and then by a rough path around Mynydd Carnguwch, a hill, like so many hereabouts, topped with Iron Age hut circles. From there to Bodfuan, on tracks to Dinas and Llaniestyn, to Sarn and across open country on Mynydd

Rhiw. From there there is a substantial grass verge to a minor road through Rhoshirwaun to Ysgubor Bach and thence by lane and path to the point on Mynydd Mawr on the National Trust land which overlooks Bardsey Sound.

It would, of course, be possible to ride selected parts of the Pilgrims' Ride, but for the enterprising the whole route, though challenging, is quite feasible. Careful planning is essential, but there are plenty of stopping places offering hospitality to riders and their horses. It seems clear that the establishment of the Pilgrims' Ride is closely tied in

OS Maps: 123, 115, 116, 117.

Accommodation with stables:
Mrs P. Skidmore, Ffarm Cyrnan, Waunfawr, Gwynedd, Tel: 0286 85608. Mrs M. Wroe, Siriol, Waunfawr, Gwynedd. Tel: 0286 85533. Captain and Mrs Hartley Edwards, Tyn Rhos, Chwilog, near Pwllheli, Gwynedd. Tel: 0766 88593. Mrs Renei Z. Thomas, Snowdonia Riding Stables, Waunfawr, Gwynedd. Tel: 0286 85342. Wynnstay Equestrian Service, 63 Clawwd Poncen, Clwyd LL21 9RT. Tel: 0490 2076. Mrs S. Roberts, Cein y Fedw Farm, Pen y Bryn, Pen y Cae, Wrexham. Tyn Lon Riding Centre, Llangybi, Pwllheli, Gwynedd LL53 6TB. Tel: Chwilog 618. Golden Pheasant Riding Centre, Tal-y-Garth Farm, Glyn Ceiriog, Llangollen, Clwyd LL20 7AB. Tel: 0691 72408.

Vets:
Strachan & Wignall, Tyddyn St Veterinary Surgery, Tyddyn St, Mold, Clwyd. Tel: 0352 3340/2973. G. M. Jenkins BVSc MRCVS, Llwynteg, Bryncrug, Tywyn, Meirioneth, Gwynedd LL36 9NU. Tel: 0654 710416. P. J. Pinder, Summer Villa, Penmaenmawr Road, Llanfairfechan, Gwynedd LL33 0NY. Tel: 0248 680037.

Farriers:
Ian Gareth Hughes, Smithy Cottage, Village Road, Nercwys, Mold, Clwyd. Tel: Mold 58524. E. P. Roberts DWCF, 5 Church View, Nercwys, Mold, Clwyd CH7 4ET. Tel: 0352 59637. R. M. Ellis DWCF, Cambrian Forge, Garndolbenmaen, Gwynedd LL51 9RX. Tel: Garndolbenmaen 734.

Further Help:
Mrs Daphne Tilley, British Horse Society, Blas Isaf, Bryn Rhyd yr Arian, Llansannan, near Denbigh, Clwyd. Tel: 0745 77227.

with the progress of improving the bridle-ways network through the Snowdonia National Park, which in turn would seem to be in hand. In the future it is proposed to develop a series of loops off to create one day rides. The Welsh councils involved regard the Pilgrims' Ride as important as the Pennine Way for Horses is to the English (Oh that they *were* important to the English!). It is hoped that the two projects could join with the route through Cheshire. It could certainly link with the Monks' Trod and Glyndŵr's Way.

The Pennine Way for Horses

This is the big one: a route to run parallel to the 270 mile Pennine Way for walkers, with as many circular rides off the backbone as possible. The Countryside Commission has appointed two people to do a feasibility study, following previous research by Lady Kirk and Mr Alan Kind in 1987 which identified a corridor that the way could pass. If general opinion is anything to go by, this means that an established, waymarked route is some years off, though the Countryside Commission's report is due in October 1990. The walker's route took some 30 years to become established. The problem lies not only in the permission required from the hundreds of consecutive landowners along the way to link existing bridleways, but the need for proper stabling and accommodation, though the ancient stone barns on the route may be ideal for this purpose.

However, the great work of the organizer of the recent Pony Express relay ride down both sides of the Pennines has done much to raise local consciousness. The routes chosen for this were from Gretna and Once Brewed in Northumbria down to Ashbourne in Derbyshire. It was done as a serious piece of research and adventure, but it is early days yet. The only sections really worth riding are those in the areas already covered in this book: the Peak District, the Yorkshire Dales and the Northumberland National Parks. Of these the 25 miles from Kettlewell to Bank Newton, and the 35 miles from Charlesworth to Ashbourne are well-signed and good going. Most other sections of the way are not signed and much more difficult riding. At least there is an embryo Pennine bridleway.

The Pennine Way for Horses will start on the High Peak and Tissington Trails of the White Peak in Derbyshire. Work is also being carried out on a link to the Oxway at Great Barrington, which in turn links with other long-distance bridleways in the southern counties. It will continue on from Parsley Hay through the harsh gritstone of the Dark Peak, a route across more exposed moorland than further south.

It will run between the mills and works of Manchester and Huddersfield, Halifax and Burnley. The textile industry began with the sheep and the spinning of yarn. In the eighteenth century machines were invented which could run from a watermill, and in

Dovedale, near Ashbourne in Derbyshire, close to the start of the Pennine Way for Horses.

the nineteenth century from steam. The West Riding had coal and water in abundance, the constituent ingredients of both of these forms of power. There are now 30,000 looms in these industrial towns.

It should reach into Brontë Country. Haworth, near Keighley, where the remarkable sister novelists Charlotte, Emily and Anne lived between 1820 and 1861, is almost as visited as Stratford-upon-Avon. The walkers' route comes to Haworth from the ruins of Top Withens Farm, which was the basis for the Earnshaw House in Charlotte's *Wuthering Heights*. The Parsonage, where they used to live with their father, in the little manufacturing town is now the Brontë museum.

Up the backbone of England, and after Skipton you will enter the Yorkshire Dales, leaving the heather moors of the south for the bright green sheep-clipped grass-covered grey limestone hills of the North Riding. The two Pony Express rides which have run parallel up to now split as they leave the Yorkshire Dales. The Western one goes up through the little known but extremely beautiful east Cumbria, always dwarfed by its Lake District sister, to finish at Gretna.

The other goes through County Durham into Northumberland where the commercial organization High Pennine Rides have negotiated several routes on the rough tracks and moorland paths of Durham, Northumbria and Cumbria, mostly areas of outstanding Natural Beauty. Based in Lanchester, Durham, one of the organizers is Susan Rogers, also Countryside Commission appointee to the Pennine Bridleway feasibility study, and BHS officer for Durham. Their rides range from 50 miles over three days to 100 miles over six days. You go unaccompanied, though you are provided with route cards, and stabling and accommodation is booked in advance.

The Pennine Way for Horses itself, if it follows this eastern route, will eventually go over Hadrian's Wall and into the Northumberland National Park and the Kielder Forest. At the border it will link with Dere Street.

The Greg Hut Bothy between Kirkland and Garrigill. (Picture courtesy of the Cumbria Bridleways Society/ T. P. Fell)

OS Maps: 119, 110, 109, 103, 98, 91, 86, 80, 74.

Further Help:

Mrs Susan Rogers (also BHS officer for Durham), Pennine Bridleway Project Officer (Northern), c/o Cumbria County Council, Area Manager's Office, Skirsgill Highways Department, Penrith CA10 2BQ. Tel: 0768 63747. Mr David Sykes, Pennine Bridleway Project Officer (Southern), c/o Derbyshire County Council, Highway's Department, Sheffield Road, Chapel-en-le-Frith SK12 6PQ. Tel: 0298 814621. Mrs Mary Towneley, Organizer, Pennine Pony Express, Dyneley, near Burnley, Lancashire BB11 3RE. Tel: 0282 23322.

Southern Upland Way

This was Britain's first coast to coast long distance footpath, and stretches 212 miles from Portpatrick on the Dumfries and Galloway coast to Cockburnspath on the eastern seaboard. Dumfries and Galloway Regional Council point out that 'No provision was made for horse riding. The route is, in any case, totally impracticable from a riders point of view' citing stiles across fences and locked gates. A proprietor of stables in the Galashiels area said that, 'There have been suggestions about opening this (way) up, but farmers tend to be nervous about hunt gates that get left open. The "Way" in this part of Scotland (Borders region) would be ideal as a ride... it is just sad we seem unable to do more about it all.'

However, the Countryside Commission for Scotland's brochure for the walker's route mentions '7 and 14 trekking holidays on the Southern Upland Way', and at least one riding centre is established there, in Beattock, and advertised by the Dumfries and Galloway Tourist Board. The Countryside Commission there are sounding out local councils and others with a view to the future provision of more riding, and the BHS themselves have attempted to give the needs of riders a higher profile than before, so it seems the need for more official organization of routes is being felt. This is the least likely of these proposed routes to be put into practice in the foreseeable future, which is a shame, because the country it crosses is some of the horsiest territory in the British Isles.

The Glen of Trool in Galloway. (J. C. Ticehurst)

Acknowledgements

Dartmoor: Sue Eberle, Jane Cox, Diana Coaker, Mrs R. Hooley, Margaret Hares, Ruth Parnell, R. E. Boulter.

Exmoor: Alexandra Rose, Helen Bingham, Alison Kent, Dawn Metrevors, Mr C. Steven, Nigel Lenton, Judy Robinson, Mrs Cody-Boutcher, Sally Heutt, Marion Balman, Ken Pettit, Rose Dyer.

The Wiltshire Droves (the Oxdrove and the Herepath): Elizabeth Hinings, Adrian Moyes, Linda Jewell.

The Ridgeway: Penny Reid, Jos Joslin, D. G. Venner, Mrs Skinner.

The Swan's Way: Robert Wood, Brenda Wickham, Kate Day, A. Turner, Sylvia Stanier, Nan Girling.

The South Downs Way: Mrs C. White, W. E. Adams, Mrs V. Perrin, Mr Campbell, Charles Shippam, Bill Bide, Phil Belden, R. Luffman, Paul Millmore, M. A. Ashton.

The Downs Link Path: Jane Edwards, Mrs C. White, Mrs J. Miller, Julia Martin, Mr Sparrow.

The Peddar's Way: Jean Taylor, Mrs Gould, Mrs Cleasby-Thompson, Mrs Bates.

Peak District National Park (the High Peak Trail and the Tissington Trail): Mrs E. Andrews, Andrew Greenwood, Harry Cowley, A. G. Harrop, Angie Rann, Shirley Walters.

The Yorkshire Dales: Mrs A. Roberts, John Conway.

The Lake District: Mrs W. Joan Chapman, Mrs T. P. Fell, Derek Robinson, Mike Pearson, Lynne Potter.

Northumberland (Clennel Street and the Salter's Road): J. F. Ogilvie, Patrick Whitehead, T. Clubley, Elspeth Davison, Mr R. Philipson.

Dere Street and Hawick Circular Ride: Mrs Ann Fraser, Mrs M. Shiel, C. Buist, Quentin McClaren.

Glyndŵr's Way: P. Wharton, F. D. Keast, Miss M. E. Cookson, Daphne Tilley, Mrs Jacqui Brown.

The Southern Cambrians (the Monks' Trod): David Bown, Sally Roberts, Mandy Prichard, Julia Dix, Avril Henn, Mrs J. B. Gibbins.

Brecon Beacons: Joe Bryant, Michael Turner.

Proposed Bridleways: W. A. Bowes, H. Anderson, Tony Hogarth, J. O. Lazarus, Dr Lisa Hooper, P. Eyton-Jones, John Simons, Mary Towneley, Susan Rogers, Judith Lund, Rosemary Cope, David Newbegin, Christine Delver, G. F. Grime, P. J. Johnson, F. N. Taylor, Chris Sainty, Mrs Brenda Wickham, Bill Bide, Daphne Tilley, Mrs Penelope Reid, Donald Pearse, Renei Thomas.

General: Paul Lister, Sandra Boothman, Chris Gledhill, K. Adsett, K. P. King, Dr R. Gritton, Nic Wheeler, Sue Scourfield, Mrs Y. Walker, John Sugden, Mrs J. Cook, Mrs Dick, Peter Dobey, S. Church, Lindsey Bedford, Wendy Dunham, Julia Thorn and Peter Fitzmaurice.